Gifts for the Journey

Gifts for the Journey

TREASURES OF THE CHRISTIAN LIFE

M. Scott Peck, M.D.,
and Marilyn von Waldner

Previously published as
What Return Can I Make?:
Dimensions of the Christian Experience

HarperSanFrancisco
A Division of HarperCollins*Publishers*

Credits appear on page 155.

GIFTS FOR THE JOURNEY: *Treasures of the Christian Life*. Text copyright © 1985, 1995 by M. Scott Peck. Lyrics copyright © 1979 by Monastery of Discalced Carmelites. All rights reserved. Printed in Hong Kong. No part of this book may be used or reproduced in any manner whatsoever without written permission except in the case of brief quotations embodied in critical articles and reviews. For information address HarperCollins Publishers, 10 East 53rd Street, New York, NY 10022.

FIRST HARPERCOLLINS EDITION PUBLISHED IN 1995.

Library of Congress Cataloging-in-Publication Data

Peck, M. Scott (Morgan Scott), 1936–
        Gifts for the journey : treasures of the Christian life / by M.
    Scott Peck and Marilyn von Waldner.
            p.   cm.
        Rev. ed. of: What return can I make?
        Includes bibliographical references.
        ISBN 0-06-066448-7
        1. Christian life.   I. Von Waldner, Marilyn.   II. Peck, M. Scott
(Morgan Scott), 1936–   What return can I make?   III. Title.
BV4501.2.P3638   1995
248.4—dc20   95-8245
                                                                          CIP

ISBN 0-06-066448-7 (pbk)

95 96 97 98 99 HCP-HK 10 9 8 7 6 5 4 3 2 1

This edition is printed on acid-free paper that meets the American National Standards Institute Z39.48 Standard.

This work is dedicated to the Glory of God

Contents

Preface to the HarperCollins Edition

I AM GRATEFUL to the readers of the first edition of this work—originally entitled *What Return Can I Make?: Dimensions of the Christian Experience*—who have long sought its republication, and to HarperCollins for obliging them and me with this new edition.

The art and sheet music that were present in the first edition have been deleted in this republication so as to create a more approachable and affordable package.

The title and subtitle have been changed to *Gifts for the Journey: Treasures of the Christian Life*. These changes seem to better capture the essence of the work as a whole. Alterations in the text of this new edition, however, are minimal.

A dozen years ago when I first wrote these meditations to Marilyn von Waldner's music I was a "baby Christian," filled with the joy of the newly converted. Old-timers warned me the honeymoon would pass with the years, and they were correct. Age, illness, frustration, and plain fatigue have taken a certain toll, and today I might best be called a "slightly jaded Christian."

So it is that when I reread my words herein, now further along the road I have traveled, I am struck by the freshness of the faith that they convey. Nonetheless, what I wrote back then remains true. Although my mood today may be less uplifted, my faith has in no way become diminished or changed in any sense other than deepened. I still believe with Marilyn that "The Lord is my light and my salvation." Moreover, as my body becomes more decrepit, as I find myself able to *do* less and my physical death looms closer, I echo Marilyn's lyrics more fervently than ever:

> To wait for my God with courage is my hope.
> Give me Your courage, Lord.
> Help me wait for You.

Introduction

IN THE SPRING OF 1977, having completed the first draft of *The Road Less Traveled*, I felt I had earned a vacation. It was to be a perfectly selfish gift to myself. I did not want to spend it with my family. I wanted to go where I wanted to go, do what I wanted to do. But where and what was that? I enjoyed traveling to foreign lands, but not alone. Simply lying on a beach somewhere seemed somehow empty, meaningless. It was at this point that I became taken with a novel sort of fancy. Why not go off to visit a Christian monastery for a few weeks? That surely was different. God knew what it would be like. But that would be the point of it; it would be an adventure. My own little adventure.

I thought of it as something exotic—if not quixotic. Little did I realize that I was embarking upon an ancient, well-trodden path.

Any educated person knows of the central role played by convents and monasteries in medieval society. Few, however, think of monastic life as being particularly relevant today. But the fact is that these places serve the late twentieth century in the same ways they served the twelfth: as centers of knowledge, where the "light" is kept alive amid the "darkness"; as places of gentle, nurturing hospitality and guidance for spiritual travelers; as foci where the battle between good and evil is most vigorously joined with prayer.

Blindly, then, I stumbled (or, stumbling, I was led) into a fresh but ancient world of daily offices—matins, diurnum, vespers, compline—of new twists to old words—*contemplative, community, vocation*—of feast days and spiritual directors, postulants and novices; a world where solitude was respected and silence regarded as something to be sought after rather than avoided. It felt right, this world. In contradistinction to my stereotypes, it was a world of much tension, and I learned that monks and nuns have not yet cornered the market on saintliness. But it was the right place at the right time for me. Christian doctrine and practice began to seem less alien.

Two years later, when I was still dragging my feet toward making a "Christian commitment," my life became further enriched by virtue of the "monastic connection." On an obscure piece of monastic literature, I spied an advertisement for a record by Sister Marilyn von Waldner, O.C.D. It was entitled "What Return Can I Make?" and subtitled "Songs of the Barrington Carmel." Interested in matters monastic, I sent away for it. Once again, it was the right thing at the right time.

Sister Marilyn's music spoke to me. Her songs elucidated my own feelings and dim comprehensions. Alternately—and sometimes simultaneously—her music inspired and consoled me. And I needed consolation. The spiritual journey is not always easy. One of its trials may be the fear of insanity. There were many moments, as I began talking more and more intimately with God (or was it to myself?) and actually relating to a man—Jesus—who had been dead for more than nineteen centuries, when I won-dered if I was not losing my mind. But the spirit of Marilyn's music and her condensed, often biblical lyrics seemed to me to capture the essential dimensions of Christianity. Certainly they captured the dimensions of my own personal religious experience. Affirmed, consoled, and encouraged, I moved forward, deeper into my strange new faith.

I wrote Marilyn a letter of gratitude and asked for five more copies. Then ten more. Later I asked for nearly a hundred of her records and distributed them to selected patients and friends across the country. Why? What would cause someone to purchase so many copies of a single record? Insanity? The fact is that once we human beings become willing to be "crazy for God," we become ever more eager to turn others on to our holy madness.

I suppose this compulsion to "turn others on" is characteristic of altered states of consciousness. Once we have seen the world in a dramatically different light—as we may do through drugs ranging all the way from alcohol to LSD—we desperately want to share our new perceptions. But the new vision that results from a Christian conversion is vastly different from drug-induced experiences. Although its intensity may wax and wane, the Christian vision is not a fleeting experience, lasting only as long as a drug remains in the bloodstream. It usually lasts a lifetime. And while the individual under the influence of a drug may find extraordinary new meaning in ordinary experience, such as the petal of a flower or the twist of a phrase, there is no particular coherence to such visions. The Christian vision, on the other hand, is a coherent one; it does not just illuminate ordinary experience, but suffuses with meaning the entirety of evolution and the whole of human existence, even on a day-to-day level.

So it is natural—even inevitable—that we should want to turn others on to a vision often so completely and constantly thrilling. It is simply impossible for the genuine—i.e., enthusiastic—Christian not to be an evangelist. But how do you turn someone on to an entirely new way of seeing the world, when there isn't a pill to alter the brain's biochemistry on behalf of the transformation?

The temptation is to turn others on by rational argument. Many fall into it. It seems appropriate to attempt to persuade by logic when the logic of the Christian vision is so utterly compelling. The problem is that this logic is compelling only to those who already have the faith. There are indeed proofs of the reality of God. But to those who live within a godless state of mind, such proofs sound like so much empty noise.

No, the transformation begins not in the mind, but in the heart. And if the heart is "hardened," no words can penetrate it. Conversely, when one has undergone what the Old Testament Jews aptly called a "circumcision of the heart," the words of the gospel message may fall upon the mind like the sweetest drops of living water.[1] Somehow, then, the successful evangelist must speak to the heart.

This is why I became such an eager distributor of Marilyn's music. It speaks to the heart. At the same time, however, I became aware of a most interesting phenomenon. While many listeners acknowledged that their hearts responded to the music, it seems their minds rejected its spiritual meaning. "I liked the songs," one person commented. "I found myself wanting to dance. She sure

---

1. Deuteronomy 30:6.

sings well. But frankly, I also found them a bit silly. The lyrics were what turned me off. It's so childish. I'm glad that she's got her faith. I mean, she really seems to believe in what she's singing, and she clearly is a joyous person. But as far as I am concerned, all that Jesus-loves-you stuff is sickeningly sweet and too simplistic for me to take."

I think that this divorce between the head and heart, between intellect and emotion, is a common spiritual condition among sophisticated twentieth-century men and women. I find many people to be Christians in their hearts while they are simultaneously intellectual atheists. It is truly a pity. These people—generous, gentle, honest, and dedicated to their fellow human beings—are often filled with despair, finding little meaning in existence, while at the same time denying the joyful or soothing voices of their heart, labeling the heart's message as "sentimental," "unrealistic," or "childish." Lacking faith in their innermost selves, they are hurting unnecessarily.

Thinking how I might help such people to whom I had given Marilyn's record, I found myself mentally devising commentaries that might bridge the gap between the head and the heart. Gradually a multidimensional celebration developed in my mind. Marilyn agreed to be its co-creator.

At the time she wrote this music Marilyn was a nun in the Order of Carmelites Discalced. The Carmelite order traces its origin to a group of men and women who lived in solitude on the slopes of Mount Carmel in Palestine from even before the time of Christ.

The reason these people chose a life of solitude was that they were contemplatives. A contemplative is a person whose deepest desire is to exist in the closest possible relationship to God. Nothing else matters much. As Marilyn sings:

> One thing I ask my God and this I seek
> To spend my whole life in your presence, Lord;
> To ponder your goodness, Lord, for all my days;
> Be guided by you. Please guide me, Lord.

Everyone exists in a relationship to God—whether he or she likes it or not. Indeed, many spend their days trying to run away from God. But the fact that it is a running-away relationship does not alter the fact that it is still a relationship (even if a negative one).

The contemplative desires in his or her heart to move in the direction toward God and ever deeper into His embrace. This cannot be done without the benefit of solitude. It is simply impossible to remember, much less listen to, what is truly important and real when one is in the midst of unending noise. Thus those who seek to flee God (and, therefore, themselves) will often be terrified by being alone and will frantically seek, at all costs, company, activity, "amusement," and external stimulation.

The contemplative, on the other hand, likes to be quiet and alone a good deal of the time. So also may those whom psychiatrists label "schizoid": persons who avoid all relationships—whether with God or with other humans—because they fear any relationship carries with it pain. The guiding motive of the contemplative, however, is not to turn away from people, but to turn toward God. The contemplative is not afraid of being hurt by relationships. To the contrary, he or she knows of

that internal rending called "the broken heart," which is the especial lot of all sensitive people. Any such person does not live long in this world before the heart is broken. Then as life goes on, the broken heart will be further sundered into smaller and ever smaller pieces. This is especially the case, of course, with those who deliberately seek union with him, whose heart the world insisted upon breaking one more time even after he died. . . . However, they also come to know that, without any question, the important thing is to let the world break the human heart. For one thing, there is room in the broken heart—and only there—for all the sorrows of the world. The broken heart—and only it—is curative, redemptive, of the wasteland around. In addition, it is the very raw material necessary for a strange and important alchemy, which has been described in the words "Your sorrow shall be turned into joy"(John 16:20).[2]

So contemplatives are not necessarily isolated persons. It is, in fact, not possible to passionately love God and not also passionately love people. But the passion of contemplatives is a quiet kind—thoughtful and prayerful.

As the centuries passed, the contemplative discipline of the Carmelite monks and nuns became lax. Reform was initiated in the middle of the sixteenth century by the great saint Teresa of

2. Gale D. Webbe, *The Night and Nothing* (San Francisco: Harper & Row, 1983), pp. 61–62.

Ávila. Because of their return to a vow of poverty, which Teresa insisted upon, the reformed Carmelites came to be referred to as "discalced" or "shoeless."

Contemplation is not a uniquely Christian activity. Indeed, I was a contemplative long before I had the slightest interest in Christ. Hasidic, Sufi, and Zen Buddhist contemplative traditions provided my primary spiritual sustenance during late adolescence and young adulthood and paved my way with their smooth wisdom. Even when I was a child, my well-meaning but sometimes thoughtless parents used to regularly say to me, "Scotty, you think too much." What a silly thing to say to someone if you contemplate the matter!

After I went to the convent (not Marilyn's, but an Episcopal one) for that first retreat, I selected, by God's grace, one of the nuns to be my spiritual director. A wonderfully gentle-hard taskmaster, she assumed her duties by inquiring as to my prayer life. "Oh, I have a fine prayer life," I replied. "I pray when I'm out walking, when I'm going to sleep at night, when I'm listening to a patient and don't know what else to do. I pray lots."

"Do you set aside any particular and specific times to pray?" she asked me.

"No," I answered. "That would seem to me rather stultified, unnecessarily rigid and unspontaneous."

"Maybe so," she responded, "but what I hear you saying is that you simply pray to God whenever you feel like it, whenever it's convenient to you. That sounds like a rather one-way relationship to me, as if you are willing to relate to God only on your terms. If you love God as much as you say you do—and I suspect you do—then I think you owe it to Him to set aside some times to be available to Him whether you feel like it or not, some time that will be His and not just yours."

That was difficult to argue with. So I set about carving out of my life two hours a day when I do "nothing" (in the world's terms) other than attempt in my own inadequate way to be available to God. Initially this handing over of "my" time was not easy. But it was also not long before I began to reap benefits.

My two hours a day of doing "nothing" (divided into several shorter periods, not all at once) have become the most important hours of my day. Only by carving them out of my busyness can I possibly reflect upon what I am doing and where I might be going. Only in this way can I vaguely keep my balance. I spend roughly ten percent of this time in prayer (speaking to the external God) and ten percent in meditation (listening to the internal God) and the remaining eighty percent just thinking. One of the advantages of being an overtly religious person is that I call these two hours my "prayer time." If I called it my "contemplation time" or my "thinking time," people would be more inclined to interrupt it. But calling it my prayer time makes it sound holy (which it is, but it still helps to use the tricks of the trade).

This business of "just thinking" is not simply a matter of one's own individual life or spiritual journey. We assume that most people know how to think. But hardly! Most people haven't even learned to take the time to think. When people ask me how I can manage my complex life as a husband, father, psychotherapist, lecturer, author, and feeble do-gooder, I often tell them about the two hours a day I spend doing "nothing" except contemplation. Ironically, they usually respond that they themselves are far too busy to do this.

While contemplation is not uniquely monastic, I do not want to disparage the virtues of a relatively cloistered life. Most people would imagine the existence of a contemplative monk or nun to be a dull one, empty of worldly experience. But the opposite tends to be the case. The contemplative life is the most full and exciting one there is. What people fail to realize is that it is not the *amount* of experience that counts; it is what we do with that experience. The contemplative is able to take a relatively small amount of external stimulation or experience and milk it for all it's worth internally. As T. S. Eliot almost nastily put it, "People to whom nothing has ever happened cannot understand the unimportance of events."[3]

When one takes the time to think, thinking invariably becomes meditative. While there are some more or less esoteric techniques that may enhance meditation, the one essential element is time. For this reason, I suggest that you consider each essay and song as a single "meditation."[4] This work has not been designed for you to skim. Please take your time with it—be contemplative— and "milk it for all it's worth."

You might best do this by beginning with the heart. Start by listening to one of Marilyn's songs. Then read my accompanying intellectual meditation. Finally, return to the music. In this way

3. T. S. Eliot, *The Family Reunion* in *The Complete Poems and Plays 1909–1950* (New York: Harcourt, Brace, 1952).

4. In *The Language of Drawing* (Prentice-Hall, 1966), Edward Hill concluded: "Drawing is an act of meditation." The same can be said of music, as well as my writing.

you may find yourself putting the head and heart together—integrating the right and left sides of your brain, so to speak.

Another suggestion: Marilyn's lyrics should be understood literally. There is no need to look for metaphors in her words. I have chosen to write meditations on her lyrics precisely because they are a superb condensation of Christian theology. Being so condensed, these lyrics have little room in them for metaphor. When Marilyn sings, for instance, "The Lord is my light and my salvation," she does not mean the Lord's Presence is like a light or that it has served her as a kind of salvation. She means just what she says. And so do I. We mean exactly and unequivocally that the Lord is our light and our salvation. May the Lord also be yours.

While there is only one Lord, each of us must approach Him and be approached by Him through the context of our own utterly unique individual limitations, gifts, and experience. While this is intended to be a work of evangelism—and it is often those who already consider themselves Christians who most need to be evangelized—it is not intended to say that our way must be your way.

It was the contemplation of my unique experience over the years that led me to conclude for myself that Christian doctrine was not a collection of imagined fables and wishful thinking, but the most penetratingly accurate approach I know to the way things really are. Ever so gradually and against virtually all of my intellectual instincts, I came through reflection on the particular happenings of my life to personally discover the incredibly wonderful Judeo-Christian God of Presence—a God who is actively present, every minute, in the here and now—a very active, living, and suffering God, who personally loves me and all His creatures. And, as if that were not enough, even more slowly it began to dawn on me that this marvelous God was indeed inextricably interwoven with the human Jesus.

Since this work is so definitely Christian, it will probably be primarily read and listened to by women and men who already identify themselves as Christians. I believe it will enrich them in their faith. But it is also very much my hope that it will be picked up by many who are not Christians. Christianity can seem a most alien doctrine to the uninitiated. For those of other traditions, this work may do much to make the strangeness of Christianity more understandable. To those who currently find little meaning in the world, and yet still yearn for it, perhaps, by God's grace, they may obtain within these pages exactly that which they have crossed the long desert to find.

M. Scott Peck, M.D.

THE LORD HAS DONE GREAT THINGS FOR US

(Based on Psalm 126)

W hen the Lord brought us home
    We were like children dreaming.
    We could not believe our good fortune.
    And our hearts were full of joy.
    We were laughing, crying,
    And all that we did was in rejoicing.
    And all we could do was sing of the Lord.

As we sang we were heard,
    And all of the people stood in wonder.
    In awe and amazement they began saying,
    "Blessed are you in your good fortune."
    So we danced and we sang,
    And all that we did was in rejoicing.
    And all we could do was sing of the Lord.

In our hearts near despair
    We'd left our own land nearly broken.
    Bearing our burden, seed for the sowing.
    Our tears in sadness would not cease.
    Now we're reaping, laughing,
    And all that we do is in rejoicing.
    And all we can do is sing of the Lord.

Now return us O Lord,
All our distress and sorrow ended.
Renew us as streams in the desert.
And fill our hearts with Your joy.
In our living, dying,
And all that we do we'll do rejoicing.
And all we can do is sing of You, Lord.

REFRAIN
The Lord has done great things for us
And we are full of joy.

1 *Conversion*

CONVERSION MEANS "TURNING WITH." Turning with what?
With God. When one is converted, one turns and begins walking with God.

But what about before our conversion? With whom were we walking then? The answer is no one. We were walking alone because we preferred it that way.

Those of us who have been converted know now that God was walking with us all the time. Only we didn't know it then, because we still thought we could go it alone. We *wanted* to go it alone. We wanted to be in charge, and because we wanted so much to be in charge, we actually believed we were. And because we believed we were in charge, we could not see God—except sometimes perhaps at a very great distance and never close enough to actually experience Him as *real*.

An alcoholic executive had been attending Alcoholics Anonymous meetings for six months but sought my help because "AA wasn't working." He had memorized the Twelve Steps, he informed me, yet for every night he went to an AA meeting he spent another night blind drunk. I suggested that the Twelve

Steps—simple though they sounded—constituted a body of profound spiritual wisdom, which took at least several years to understand. He acknowledged that the steps didn't mean much to him, particularly all that "stuff about putting trust in a Higher Power." But he proclaimed he certainly understood the First Step: "I admit that I am powerless over alcohol." I asked him what he thought it meant.

"It's simple," he replied. "It means that once I take a drink the alcohol takes over. Once I start I can't help myself. It means I can't take that first drink."

"Then how is it that you are still drinking?" I asked.

He looked nonplused for a moment. "I guess I just don't have the willpower."

"Maybe that's what the First Step really means," I suggested. "Maybe it means not only that you are powerless after you've taken a drink, but that you alone are powerless even before you've taken the first drink."

"That's not true," he exclaimed. "It's up to me. I'm a competent person. I can determine whether or not I'm going to take that first drink."

"That's what you feel, but it's not how you act."

"It's still all up to me," he insisted.

"Have it your way," I said.

Most of us enter adolescence or adulthood like that alcoholic, believing ourselves to be "our own person." To an extent this is good. It is good that we should take responsibility for ourselves and have what psychiatrists call a "sense of autonomy." It is, in fact, an essential foundation for spiritual growth. But there is a subtle yet crucial point beyond which we cannot "go it alone" successfully—beyond which a sense of self-determination not only becomes prideful and begins to interfere with further spiritual growth but also denies reality.

The reality is that we are all being manipulated by a "higher power." Free will allows us to deny the manipulation, fight against it, or cooperate with it. Before we can choose to cooperate, it is, of course, necessary to realize that the source of the "manipulation" is not only an intelligence far greater than our own, but also one that clearly has our best interests at heart. This realization and the subsequent decision to cooperate—to acquiesce—is the process of conversion.

The essential turning point in the conversion process, then, is the new understanding that the ego of the individual—though it is important—is not King. The King is the Lord God. But the ego is not easily dethroned. A very real sort of ego death is required. In order that this death may occur, the individual spirit must first be broken in some way. "Our hearts near despair, we'd left our own land nearly broken," sings Marilyn of this transition. I would go her one better. Marilyn *was* broken. She had to be to sing her songs.

This brokenness is the ego death symbolized by the drowning of sin in baptism. The death of which Christ spoke when he said, "Whosoever shall lose his life shall save it," occurs in many different ways. For myself it was mercifully slow, taking place in gentle stages over a dozen years. For others it may come through weeks or months of illness or other agonizing suffering. For still others it may come suddenly, like a searing flash of pure blazing pain.

If it comes at all. Many will never be broken—at least not until physical death. There are a number of reasons for this, some of which we do not understand. Certainly it is understandable that we should not want to die before our time, no matter what promises Jesus might hold out to us. Nevertheless, as a wise priest said to me when I was dragging my feet over becoming baptized, "We all have to die sooner or later; why not get on with it?"

But I would like to single out one reason for our refusal to be broken. It is our distaste—indeed, our fear—to be "as children." Here we have made it into adulthood. We are parents and authorities, hardheaded scientists and businesspeople, directing banks and corporations and trust funds and programs. How are we now to suddenly turn around and say, in effect, "Daddy, please give me my allowance." Finally free from the often destructive domination of our biological fathers, why should we now turn our gaze upward toward something invisible and, with a sense of absolute powerlessness, ask, "Father . . ."? And, reduced to a state of seeming dependency, why make that invisible something our Lord and Master? Dammit, haven't we learned how to take care of ourselves?

But Jesus could not have been more clear on this point. "Except ye be converted," he said, "and become as little children, ye shall not enter into the kingdom of heaven. Whosoever therefore shall humble himself as this little child, the same is greatest in the kingdom of heaven."[5]

So it is no accident that Marilyn sings, "When the Lord brought us home, we were like children dreaming." He could not bring us home until we were like children, willing to be led and willing to put our trust in the benignity of the invisible, intangible, unknowable God.

5. Matthew 18:3–4.

But when we do place our trust in God, we come home. Home is the kingdom of heaven; it is where we belong, where we were meant to be. The kingdom, of course, is not a place in the materialistic sense; it is a state of mind. When we achieve that state of mind through conversion we realize that we have not "died" at all; we feel as if we were more alive than ever. What we took to be a dream turns out to be reality, and we see clearly for the first time. The kingdom—this state of mind—feels so *right*. The kingdom is reality; it is where our mind belongs. We have, indeed, come home.

One of the remarkable things about the conversion experience is its commonality. By this I do not mean the experience is common in the sense of ordinary. To the contrary, if it occurs at all it does so completely once in a lifetime. But having occurred, the conversion experience is predictable; it obeys certain laws. Whether one comes to the experience from poverty or wealth, from ignorance or erudition, in youth or in old age, whether it happens suddenly or gradually, the experience is always the same. No matter how different the means of our breaking may be, the brokenness always occurs. And no matter which path one has traveled to conversion, the experience is invariably one of great joy, once the breaking is all over. You can sense this joy in Marilyn's music. And her joy is also mine.

Now I must make some corrections. I have spoken of conversion as if it were a single, sudden event. It merely seems that way for some. I mentioned that my own breaking took place in gentle stages—as if God knew I couldn't take much pain. There are those who can say, "It happened at eight-thirty on the night of the seventeenth of August." But if asked I would have to respond like psychologist Paul Vitz, author of *Psychology as Religion*, who when asked at a lecture when he became a Christian, scratched his head for a moment and replied, "Let's see; it was sometime between '72 and '76."[6]

Actually, conversion is always a process. The person whom God reached down and touched at eight-thirty on the night of the seventeenth of August may spend the rest of her or his life undergoing a "softening of the heart" and being converted to peace and injustice as a result of that touching. An atheist, on the other hand, may long ago have had his heart "circumcised." All that remains is the conversion of his intellect. Yet even then the conversion process will continue. Marilyn and I can each tell you that our conversions are continuing to deepen as we continue to undergo little breakings and little deaths and pass "from glory to glory."[7]

I have also written about the conversion experience as if it were something that we can *achieve.* I have done this because I believe there are specific ways in which we may by choice prepare and be open to the experience, thereby deliberately cooperating with God's design. Yet the reality of the situation is that we cannot be converted simply through our own efforts. Something more is needed to "break through our egotistical barriers."[8] Obviously, we do not come to the knowledge that we cannot go it alone by going

6.   There are two different stages in religious development. The scholar currently known best for his work on this subject is James W. Fowler, author of *Stages of Faith: The Psychology of Human Development and the Quest for Meaning* (San Francisco: Harper & Row, 1981).

7.   2 Corinthians 3:13.

8.   Janie Gustafson, *Celibate Passion* (New York: Harper & Row, 1978), p. 46.

it alone. We need—and receive—supernatural help. This is the reason why another common feature of the conversion experience is the sense of its extraordinary nature. Converts do not feel that they have earned or achieved something; rather they feel that something extraordinary has happened to them. We know that God has somehow—through His grace—intervened in our lives. We know—children that we are—we were not smart enough to find our way home all by ourselves. The "Lord brought us home." Thank you Lord.

THE SUNSHINE OF HIS LOVE

From the center of my soul, a flower grows inside me,
A love that makes me whole, a budding love that sets me free.
And in my troubled times this warmth of life consoles me.
The sunshine of His love that heals my heart, that lets me be.

And in the springtime of my life, a gentle rain enfolds me.
To cleanse my saddened heart to refresh my labored soul.
In the sweetness of the wind, again His warmth will console me.
The sunshine of His love that heals my heart, that lets me be.

REFRAIN
My Father shines for me.
I am part of His creation.
The mystery of His love, so great none could compare.
A gentle wave of His hand,
He lifts me high upon a mountain.
And soon joy fills my heart, as from a playful mountain stream.

2 Grace

GRACE IS THE GIFT unearned, the wonderful unexpected present, the blessing undeserved. It is sunshine in a place where there is usually only darkness. It is the bursting presence of love at a time when we have the right only to expect condemnation or emptiness and aloneness.[9]

I have worried over the use of the word *manipulated* in the previous meditation on conversion. To psychotherapists, it is a dirty word. The term *manipulate* is often used to describe a type of human interaction that is inherently dishonest and uncaring. The people psychotherapists work to heal may never have known any other form of relationship, which is often why they are ill. And healing is difficult because when such patients experience genuine love for the first time they usually reject it as foreign, feeling it should not be trusted.

There is often a similar reaction when people first experience God's love. They are moved, but profoundly suspicious of the Mover. "A gentle wave of His hand," Marilyn sings, "He lifts me

9. See Robert Farrar Capon, *Between Noon and Three: A Parable of Romance, Law, and the Outrage of Grace* (San Francisco: Harper & Row, 1982).

high upon a mountain." By His hand we are jiggled like puppets. It this not manipulation? This playing with our emotions, this toying with our very lives? Indeed, it is almost proper that the human spirit should initially resent and either deny it or fight against such power.

But wait! What kind of manipulation is this when the Power is prodding us toward health and lifting us toward vision? When the Power teaches us how to be powerful? When instead of serving the Power, the Power serves us? "My Father shines for me," Marilyn's words sing. What are we to do with this illogic—we courtiers of Machiavelli, bearers of velvet-gloved fists and veiled thermonuclear threats? It makes no sense in terms of all that we have been taught by history as interpreted by our elders. My Father shines for me—indeed!

Are we, however, utterly unacquainted with such loving power? Let us consider our fathers and mothers. Although they are in the minority, the fact is that at least a few parents serve their children so thoroughly that they truly do exist for them. "They are the light of my life" is to say in such cases: "I live, exert myself still, and shine for them." Is it possible that God loves us with the same kind of parental dedication of which we are, at our best, capable?

In the sense that He actively intervenes in our lives and influences us without our even being able to begin to understand what is happening, God (like any decent human parent) is a manipulator. In that He intervenes out of concern for us and to our benefit (like any decent parent), God is not a manipulator. A care that "consoles," "heals," "refreshes," and "cleanses" cannot be considered manipulative in the negative sense of the word. And certainly not a love "that lets me be"!

In the summer of 1982, my eldest daughter and I flew from our home in northwestern Connecticut to Salt Lake City, where I had a two-day speaking engagement at a Mormon conference. I had accepted the engagement because I thought it might be an excellent opportunity for me to learn about the Mormon religion. I took my daughter with me because she was interested in the conference as well. Additionally, I thought it would be good for both of us to have a space of time together to enrich our relationship. It was a smart move. The conference did indeed turn out to be a crash course in Mormonism, and my daughter and I very much enjoyed each other's company.

Four days after our return a man called me for a consultation, and I saw him three days later. He turned out to be a Mormon who had been very much nurtured by his church and was deeply dependent upon it. At the same time he was skeptical of a number of Mormon doctrines that made him feel quite oppressed. I would have been in a poor position indeed to appreciate the depth of his dilemma had it not been for my recent education.

Now it so happens that there are precious few Mormons living in northwestern Connecticut. In fact, in my ten years of practice in the area I had never met one, much less treated one. Do you think it was an accident that one week after my crash course in Mormonism the first Mormon patient in ten years crossed the doorstep of my office?

I asked God, "Did you send me all the way out to Salt Lake City to prepare me to work with this man?" The answer seemed to be "yes," but only in part. Because what I learned there was of benefit to me as well as to my patient. Because the trip gave me the finest time I had ever spent with my daughter. Because both of us made good new friends there. The efficiency of God's "manipulation"—of His grace—never ceases to amaze me. Not a wasted motion!

The songs herein speak of a God who is actively, personally involved with us—caring, encouraging, influencing. But how is it possible for such a God to actively intervene in our lives on the one hand and "let us be" on the other? To understand this question, let us consider once again how the best parents operate. Their involvement with their children is most vigorous, yet their design is not to turn their children into carbon copies of themselves. Unlike narcissistic parents who will attempt to break a child's spirit so as to conform it to their own self-centered needs and notions, the truly loving parent will intervene only to seek to nourish the child's uniqueness. Mature, loving parents "flow with" their children, adjusting themselves to the particular child's needs rather than forcing the child to adjust to theirs. While they must help the child to submit to the realities of human existence, loving parents do not compel submission to themselves. They respect their child's individuality. They let that individuality *be*.

There is another way in which God, the Parent, in His love, lets us be. He who "with a gentle wave of His hand" can lift us "high upon a mountain" would also seem to have the power, with the simple flick of His finger, to crush us out of existence. To make us utterly conform to His will would presumably be for Him no mechanical problem. Yet it is an impossibility for Him. Here we come face to face with one of the exquisitely beautiful paradoxes of ultimate Christian reality. God does not compel us to submit to His will because it is His will that we not be compelled. God did not make us to be slaves. He made us in His image to be free. His dearest desire is that we should follow Him, but only of our own free will. So while He does indeed intervene in our lives, His intervention never takes the form of force; its only form is gentle caring. As much as God wants us to be wholly good in His image, He knows that real goodness can result solely from choice. To lead us to goodness, God must allow us the full freedom to choose evil. He lets us be. If He does have destructive power, then our God is above all else a God of loving restraint.

Sometimes I wonder if those with an image of God as Giant Cop in the Sky with a big billy club project onto Him either their own violent proclivities and need for self-control or else their negative images of parents. Sometimes I think it is not a matter of God's restraint at all. At such times I begin to suspect that God is actually incapable of acting punitively or destructively, that He is capable only of love; that He cannot destroy, He can only create.

Not long ago, a young patient casually informed me that on the preceding evening while he was driving, his car had run out of gas. From previous experience with patients, I suspected there was a problem. "Is this the first time you've ever done that?" I asked.

"Oh, no," he blandly replied.

"How often do you run out of gas?" I inquired.

"Oh, not often. Maybe three or four times a year."

"For what it's worth," I commented, "I've never run out of gas."

"Well, the problem is the gas gauge in my car," he explained. "Once it gets down to a quarter of a tank it becomes very unreliable."

"Why don't you get the gas gauge fixed, then?"

"I suppose I should."

"You really seem quite comfortable about it," I told him. "But to me it seems to be a problem that you're trying to avoid." And I left it at that.

The next week this patient drove to Boston to visit a friend who lived on Beacon Hill. At the outskirts of Boston he stopped at a gas station to ask directions. His gas gauge read a quarter full, but he did not buy gas. When he reached Beacon Hill he found it a maze of one-way streets in which he got hopelessly lost. After meandering through them for half an hour, he ran out of gas right on top of the hill. "Maybe if I coast down the hill," he thought, "it's just possible by God's grace that I'll run into a gas station."

As he coasted down the hill vehicles almost magically seemed to get out of his way. And at the bottom, sure enough, there was a gas station. Without any application of the brakes whatsoever, his car glided slowly to a stop exactly adjacent to the correct pump.

After recounting this experience, my patient concluded by saying, "So I decided to get my gas gauge fixed."

"Since the Lord seems to be taking care of you so well," I teased, "why do you bother?"

"That's just it," he replied. "I figured if God is going to go to all that trouble to help me out with a little matter that's a result of my own laziness, the least I can do for Him is to get it fixed so He can be free to worry about more important things."

Psychologists, who study how we learn, speak in terms of negative reinforcement, by which they mean punishment, and positive reinforcement, by which they mean reward such as praise or special attention. Usually they conclude that we learn better by positive rather than negative reinforcement. Certainly this seemed to be the case with my young patient. The discomfort of having his car run out of gas at night on a country road seemed to teach him nothing. On the other hand, it was the sunshine of his good fortune that finally motivated him to learn greater responsibility. Good psychologist that He is, perhaps God can work only through "positive reinforcement."

Thus far I have been explaining God's love as if there were nothing miraculous about it. But Marilyn sings also of its mystery. "My Father shines for me," she sings. Yet I know He also shines for me. What's more, He shines for you. How He does this, I do not know. As a parent I am hard put to keep shining, even with an often mediocre light, on behalf of my three children. How can God do it for five billion? God knows. He does it, but how He does it is a mystery. If you have to have *all* the answers before you can have significant faith in God, then you won't find faith in this lifetime.[10]

10. To be without faith is not a sin, and there are worse curses possible in human existence. But you might want to pay heed to the famed words of St. Augustine: "Understanding is the reward of faith. Therefore seek not to understand that you may believe, but believe that you may understand." St. Augustine, *On the Gospel of St. John XXIX*, in *The World Treasury of Religious Quotations*, Ralph L. Woods, Editor and Compiler (New York: Garland, 1966).

Until now we have been meditating on this song as if it were a song primarily about God's love for us. It is not. It is equally about our love for God. So Marilyn begins by singing of her own center as the location of "a budding love that sets me free." This is the new love of the converted for God. But how does such love set one free? It is an extremely important question. For it is freedom that we are all after, whether we know it or not. The theme of human freedom is a thread running through Marilyn's songs, and hence a major melody of this book.

Most simply put, freedom is power. And power is competence. I am talking here, of course, about spiritual freedom, power, and competence, and about these things not simply in terms of this temporal world but in terms of the larger reality. In the world's terms, Hitler was an immensely powerful man, but he was not genuinely competent and certainly not free. He was in this life fear-ridden and crazed, and he, if anyone, is damned for all eternity. The alcoholic of whom I spoke in the preceding meditation was still a relatively wealthy executive with the freedom to fly anywhere in the world and the power to hire and fire a dozen employees. Yet he was powerless over alcohol and, in his incompetent insistence upon facing his addiction alone without God, not free to conform his behavior to what he knew was right and necessary.

But how can love for God "set us free"? How can it increase our power and competence? There are actually many ways, and they will be presented as we proceed through the meditations. For the moment, let me conclude with a simple analogy to explain that love is a relationship. Although God loves us until the end of time, unless we love Him in return we have no working relationship with Him.

Seventy years ago, my mother heard a famous preacher speak of this fact in a children's sermon. (Like so many children's books, children's sermons usually have messages for adults too!) The preacher took from his pocket a pair of scissors, the two halves of which had been unscrewed. He pointed out to the children that each part by itself was rather useless. So it is with God and people, he said. Without God, human beings are not good for much. And without women and men, boys and girls, even God can't accomplish very much—a comment that may cause some theologians indigestion. But then the preacher also took from his pocket a screwdriver and proceeded to unite the two parts into a single working *pair* of scissors. "You see," he said to the children, using them to cut effortlessly through a piece of cardboard, "fastened together they have become a marvelous, competent instrument!" This is what happens when we attach ourselves to God in loving relationship to Him. As an instrument of God, we suddenly develop the power and the freedom not only to cut through our own personal problems but even to begin cutting through the evil in the world.

JESUS' LOVE

Sometimes I go through days wondering what I should do.
And then, He comes to me and says, "I love you."
　The joy my Lord brings me, the love from which life does
　　spring to me.
　Will shine for all to see.

I'd always thought myself nothing to be worthwhile.
And then He said to me, "You are my child,
My love will make you complete, put wings upon your feet;
　you'll fly.
And I will be your guide."

REFRAIN
Jesus is always with me.
Though I'll never understand His love for me,
I know that what I feel has made me free.
Jesus' love for me.

3 *Jesus*

JESUS. JESUS JEANS. The Easter bunny. Christmas carols. O come let us adore him . . . adore him.

Adore him? Now wait a minute. That's not serious, is it? Adore? We don't adore anybody or anything anymore. It's not hip; it's not cool. Oh, sure, maybe when we were entering adolescence, there was a special girl, a special boy. Puppy love. Maybe for a day or two we once adored someone. But we got over it all too quickly, and that was long ago.

It is often difficult to tell in Marilyn's songs whether God or Jesus is being addressed. Our relationship with God brings us freedom, joy, power. Jesus brings us freedom, joy, power. Which is which? Adoration for one could be equally directed to the other.

There is a reason for this confusion: Jesus is inseparable from God. It is a point of theology that we tend to forget. When we speak of Jesus as the Son of God, we acknowledge the relationship between them, but tend to think of them as distinct individual entities. After all, just as our children leave us for college and the world, cannot the son depart from the father? The reality, however, is expressed in the ancient doctrine of the Trinity. "God the Father,

God the Son, and God the Holy Spirit" means that God *is* all three. God is more than Jesus alone. He is also Father and Spirit. But He *is* the Son.

Jesus, then, is not a symbol of God, he is God, and God is Jesus. When Jesus was born, God came to earth. In Jesus, God walked among us "as one of us." God personally experienced the human condition. God knows what it is like to suffer and die. Jesus' love and God's love are the same. It is not simply Jesus that died for us. In Jesus, God actually died for us.

Virtually all basic truth is paradoxical. I am reminded of the famous professor who was queried by a student one day, "Is it correct you believe that at the core of all reality there is paradox?" "Well," responded the professor, "yes and no."

A major problem many people have in comprehending Christianity is its mass of paradox. As a highly rational person, I'm not sure I could ever have become a Christian had I first not been prepared by two decades of study in Zen Buddhism. Zen is a marvelous training school in paradox. One of my favorite light-bulb jokes (a hobby of mine) is "How many Zen Buddhists does it take to change a light bulb?" The answer: "Two; one to change the light bulb and one to *not* change the light bulb."

Jesus sometimes referred to himself as the Son of God; at other times, as the Son of Man. He was not trying to speak in riddles, but merely trying to speak the truth about himself. The reality is that Christ is both human and divine. Thus far we have been meditating on his divinity. Some Christians come to comprehend his humanity only after accepting his divinity. For me it was the other way around; I approached his divinity through his humanity.

I first seriously read the Gospels at the age of forty. Perhaps I was not able to stomach all that paradox before then. In any case, it was a good time to read them. Had you asked me a dozen years before whether Jesus was real, I would have replied, "Oh, sure, there was a real man, a historical Jesus who lived one thousand nine hundred and fifty years ago, who was undoubtedly a pretty wise person, who was executed for his troubles in the standard manner of the day—which was no worse than ways we've been executing many people, wise and not so wise, ever since—and for some reason I don't understand they happened to build a big religion around him." And I would have left his reality at that.

You see, I knew that the Gospel writers were not contemporaries of Jesus: they had never known him personally and were writing thirty or forty years after his death, and their writings were secondhand and thirdhand accounts. And in my intellectual hubris I concluded that they were deliberately mythmaking and embellishing.

But when I finally did come to seriously read the Gospels, it was with a dozen years of experience of trying, in my own small way, to be a teacher and healer. So I knew a little about teaching and healing. And with this knowledge I was thunderstruck by the reality of the man, Jesus, that I discovered in these "thirdhand" accounts.

I discovered a man who was almost continually frustrated. It is apparent on practically every page of the Gospels: "What do I have to say to you?" Jesus asks. "How many times do I have to say it? What do I have to do to get it through to you?" I discovered a man who was frequently angry, who was prejudiced on at least one occasion (although he overcame that prejudice in transcendent healing love). I discovered a man who was sad, who was scared, and who was terribly, terribly lonely. There is no more poignant expression of loneliness in all literature than "the Son of Man has no place to lay his head."

What I began to realize was that this man Jesus was so real they could not have made him up. If the Gospel writers had been into mythmaking and embellishing as I had assumed, they would have created the kind of public relations image so many Christians today are still trying to create—what my wife, Lily, calls "the wimpy Jesus": a man with a sweet, continuous smile on his face, who goes around all day patting little children on the head, who with unflappable equanimity has achieved a mellow yellow "Christ consciousness" and reached a nirvana-like *peace of mind*.

But the Jesus of the Gospels clearly did not have peace of mind as we think of it. So I began to wonder if possibly—just possibly—the Gospel writers were, for the most part, not mythmakers and embellishers, but careful and accurate reporters, dedicated to presenting a truthful and documented account of the ministry of a very strange and wonderful man they themselves hardly began to understand, but in whom they realized that heaven and earth had converged.

And that is how I began to fall in love with Jesus.

As if it were not enough to contend intellectually with a Jesus who was both human and divine, both man and God, we must also contend with the strange reality that even though he was murdered on a cross nineteen hundred and fifty years ago, here he is speaking to Marilyn in the late twentieth century. Note that in the song we are meditating on, Jesus is present. How can this be? I don't know, any more than I know how God can be present in this world. Nor does the songwriter know. "I'll never understand His love for me," she sings. It is a miracle. It is mystery.

But while we may not understand the mechanics of Jesus' or God's presence among us, we do know that they are here. Now, Is there evidence? "By their fruits you shall know them," it is said. So we know of God and Jesus by the results of their love. What are these results? Consider just one: we are alive.

Reflect for a moment on the blind ignorance of the human race. Even with all our science, in the words of Thomas Edison, "We don't begin to know one percent about ninety-nine percent of anything." Do you think it would be possible for us, stumbling around with our puerile passions, stupid prejudices, and absurd self-satisfaction to survive at all unless we were magically guided by some infinitely tender and loving hand? A young acquaintance of mine, burdened by thoughts of self-annihilating pollution and atomic holocaust, recently wrote me to ask if I thought the world was coming to an end. I responded that the world has always been coming to an end. The reason it has not come to an end is because it has been rescued daily by God. "Love makes the world go round" sounds so trite as to be silly. Yet it is the truth of our very existence—the only basic truth I know that is not a paradox. Without God's loving presence, without His ongoing daily love, and, to a lesser extent, without our own love in feeble imitation of Jesus, the world as we know it would instantly collapse. Poof!

The act of loving always requires suffering. I am sorry, but that's the way it is. If parents love their children, then they will agonize over them. It is easy to say yes to children and it is also easy to say no. What is not easy is to seriously consider the problem, to agonize over whether to say yes or no: "Yes, you may stay out until midnight" or "No, you must be in by ten-thirty." As we suffer over our children, so God suffers over us. "Only the suffering God can help," Dietrich Bonhoeffer wrote during the imprisonment that preceded his execution.[11] It is through the suffering of His love that God keeps this world turning.

Christ is known as the "Suffering Servant." Many think of Jesus, therefore, as passive, almost weak, as if the Lamb were also not a Lion. They do not realize that when he washed the feet of those who called him Lord, he began to overturn the entire social order, as he continues to overturn it today. They do not understand that the position of servant is a position of power.

My wife and I regard ourselves as our children's servants. It is for this reason that we do not expect—except in our more immature moments—any great gratitude from them. They are entitled to our service; it is our position to serve them. It is our expectation that they themselves will grow into servanthood—that having been served and having role models for service, they will be able in turn to serve their children and the world. But a servant is not a slave. A slave is someone who does whatever his or her master wants. A servant is someone who does whatever his or her master *needs*. We would hardly serve our children well if we did everything they wanted, obeyed their every whim. It is the servant who

11. Dietrich Bonhoeffer, *Letters and Papers from Prison* (New York: Macmillan, 1972), p. 361.

decides what the master needs. And wherever the decisions are made, that's where the locus of power resides.

As only a serving, suffering God will do, so only a living—a present—God can daily rescue us: a God who not only suffered and died on the cross for us many centuries ago, but a God who suffers for us today. Jesus still dies for us that we may live. Our very life depends on it.

I am a beginner Christian. It is still hard for me to realize that Jesus is truly with me. It still seems like such a fairy tale. I feel awkward and superstitious talking with him, praying to him, asking him for his help, believing that he really could be present, believing in him. But it gets easier with practice. And it works.

In the previous meditation I spoke of how our relationship with God—our love for God—helps us to freedom and power and competence. Now we can deepen the answer. One way in which God serves us and leads us into power and freedom is in the form of Jesus. When Marilyn speaks of feeling confused ("wondering what I should do") and insignificant ("nothing to be worthwhile"), something then happens. Jesus says, "I love you. You are my child."

To actually experience God/Christ's love is to experience that we are *important*. We matter. It matters whether we take that drink. It matters whether we slap our child. It matters whether we cheat on our income tax. It matters when we risk telling the truth. It matters when we go out of our way to help another. The day-to-day state of our soul *matters*. It matters because we are loved. Whether we are rich or poor, president or derelict, genius or feeble-minded, we are loved, wherever we are, whoever we are. And we will continue to be loved no matter how deep we sink or how far we flee. Because, pathetic though we may be, God/Christ died for us and still does and always will.

So what? So what if Jesus loves us? How does being important in that way help us? In her song, Marilyn wonders what she should do, and Jesus says to her, "I will be your guide." The clearest way—at least the easiest way to talk about—that Jesus' love helps us is to say that it guides us. I shall talk much more about this matter of guidance. For the moment, however, let us examine a single phenomenon. If we are puzzled and confused and do not know which way to turn, it will make a great deal of difference in our decision-making process if we consider the whole business important—if we take ourselves seriously. That is the first piece of guidance Jesus has for each of us: Take yourself seriously. That does not mean we shouldn't laugh at ourselves. To the contrary, it means we should not despair, it means there is precious little cause for sorrow. Because if God takes us seriously enough to die for us, then maybe we ought to take ourselves seriously enough to dare to joyfully think that there is meaning and importance to our existence. So thinking, our way becomes more clear.

LORD, HOW YOU MUST LOVE ME

Lord, it seems like all I know how to do is betray You.
Through all these days You've remained with me.
In so many ways You give Your life to me.

Lord, it seems I'm always falling down in my love for You.
But You lift me up, You put my hand in Yours.
You love away all my sad discourse.

Lord, someday I'll find the way to say how much I love You.
Until that time, I know You'll understand.
Because I'm weak, because I'm human.

REFRAIN
O Lord, how You must love me.
O Lord, how You must care.

4 Guilt

GUILT IS A "DOWNER." It's a sour note in the center of a sweet melody. Listen to the tone of the song of this meditation—heavy as a corpse hung against the low sky. When I first met Marilyn, I said her songs were joyful. "Joyful is the last thing I felt writing one of them," she replied. This is the one. It's a pebble in the shoe that can't be taken out, a cinder in the eye that can't be found. It's also probably the most important song in this book.

It is a song about sin.

Sin has not been a very fashionable word these past few years. It too is a "downer." We live in times when we would like to keep things gay and light, when cultured people try not to get too serious. Even many religious have joined in, often attempting to suggest that the light of truth is somehow also light to bear. It would seem the doctrine of the day is this: all that is needed in this world is a little more affirmation. *I'm OK, You're OK* was the title of one of the leading pop psychology best-sellers a few years back.

But what happens if I'm not OK?

What happens if I dream each night I'm drowning and wake up in the dark drenched in terror? What happens if I cannot enter a supermarket, movie theater, or department store without immediately being assaulted by waves of pure panic that overwhelm all my intentions and propel me trembling back outside into the parking lot? What happens if my adolescent daughter's once warm body lies in a morgue dead from an overdose and I sense I somehow had something to do with it? And what if I *know* I had something to do with it? Or, worst yet, what if I did put her there and have no knowledge of my sin? Am I OK then?

The reality is that this world is not all OK. Evil is not the figment of some medieval theologian's imagination. Auschwitz and Mylai and Jonestown are actual places where terrible things actually happened. Human evil is real.

The reality is that we do betray God and ourselves and each other. We do it routinely. The worst of us do it blatantly, even compulsively. The noblest of us do it subtly, even when we think we are trying not to do it. Whether it is done consciously or unconsciously is of no importance; the betrayal occurs. At best we are like the bumbling disciple Peter, who kept saying, "Oh Lord, you know how much I love you," and then, although he had been forewarned, thrice denied that he even knew Jesus, realizing later that he had betrayed him. Surely, if I can recount this story I too have been forewarned. Yet I continue to catch myself in my little copouts after the fact. I wonder how many more times I will fail to recognize the reality that I have sinned—a failure that is itself a sin. Only God knows.

"Lord, it seems like all I know how to do is betray You."

There are nominal Christians of a certain type who are notable for their self-righteousness and proclivity to point the finger of sin in all directions other than themselves. Few escape their aim: the neighbor who does not go to church, the parishioner who committed adultery, the man who drinks too much, the children next door, and even their own children are all targets. Such practitioners of religion have helped to give sin its bad name in recent times. But note that the songwriter is not using the concept of sin in this way at all. She is not accusing anyone else of anything. She is pointing the finger only at herself. It is her own sin she is talking about.

This genuine awareness of one's own shortcomings is what I call a "sense of personal sin." It is not pleasant—just as this song is not pleasant. It is not pleasant to be aware of oneself as a naturally lazy, ignorant, self-centered being who routinely betrays its Creator, its fellow creatures, and even its own best intentions. Yet this unpleasant sense of personal failure and inadequacy is, paradoxically, the greatest blessing a human being can possess.

"Blessed are the poor in spirit," Jesus said as he began his one full sermon. What did he mean by this opener? The song suggests the answer. It might best be called "the poor-in-spirit song." If you want to know what "poor in spirit" means, just think of this song and the way Marilyn felt when she wrote it.

But what is so great about feeling down on yourself—about having this sense of personal sin? To answer that, it might help to remember the Pharisees. According to the New Testament, they were the fat cats of Jesus' culture. They didn't feel poor in spirit. They felt that they had it all together, that they were the ones who knew the score, who deserved to be the cultural leaders in Jerusalem and throughout Israel. And they were the ones who engineered the murder of Jesus.

Some scholars believe that the role of the Pharisees in Jesus' crucifixion as described in the Gospels is an anti-Semitic distortion. Whether or not that is the case I do not know. What I do know is that all cultures, Christian or not, including our own today, have their "Pharisees" who, self-righteously, continue to engineer the murder of multitudes either physically or emotionally. The poor in spirit do not commit evil. Evil is not committed by people who feel uncertain about their righteousness, who question their own motives, who worry about betraying themselves. The evil in this world is committed by the spiritual fat cats who think that they are without sin because they are unwilling to suffer the discomfort of significant self-examination.

Unpleasant though it may be, the sense of personal sin is precisely that which keeps our sin from getting out of hand. It is quite painful at times, but it is a very great blessing because it is our one and only effective safeguard against our own proclivity for evil. St. Thérèse of Lisieux put it so nicely in her gentle way: "If you are willing to serenely bear the trial of being displeasing to yourself, you will be for Jesus a pleasant place of shelter."[12]

Little, if anything, is usually accomplished by attempting to distinguish between "good" Christians and "bad" Christians or between true and false Christians. Yet it is hard to imagine how someone could be a genuine Christian who lacks, as many do, a sense of his or her own personal sin—who is not "for Jesus a pleasant place of shelter." It is a basic Christian doctrine that we are all sinners. By "all" we do not mean everyone other than our-

12. *Collected Letters of St. Thérèse of Lisieux*, translated by F. J. Sheed (Fairway, KS: Sheed & Ward, 1949), p. 303.

selves; we mean everyone, but primarily ourselves. The major prerequisite for membership in the True Christian Club is the self-
acknowledgment of sin. Housecleaning, like charity, should begin
at home, and we usually have quite enough to do being our own
watchdog without having to be anyone else's.

Nor should we take pride in our sense of personal sin. It is true
that those of us who have this sense are blessed—particularly in
comparison with those who don't. But the sense of sin is not something that we earn. Like all blessings, it is a gift from God. Such
gifts are given not because we deserve them, but because they are
in accord with the plan of God's grace, which is mysterious and
beyond our understanding. It is easy to hate the Pharisees of this
world, but the reality is that they are simply less fortunate than
the poor in spirit.

The Christian doctrine of sin is hardly as gloomy as many are
apt to believe. To the contrary, it is an extraordinarily gentle teaching with the happiest of endings. For whenever we experience contrition—the experience of being displeased with oneself of which
St. Thérèse spoke—we are forgiven. And nowhere is the sweet
beauty of forgiveness better described than in the following story,
given to me by a friend, of a little Filipino girl who talked to Jesus.

The word began to get around a village in the Philippines that
a little girl there talked to Jesus, and the people of this village
became excited. Then the word spread to the surrounding villages,
and more people became excited. Finally, the word reached the
cardinal's palace in Manila, and a monsignor was appointed to
investigate the phenomenon. So the girl was summoned to the
palace for a series of interviews. At the end of the third interview
the monsignor felt ready to throw up his hands. "I don't know

whether you're for real or not," he exclaimed in frustration. "But there is one acid test. This next week when you talk to Jesus, I want you to ask him what I confessed at my last confession."

The little girl agreed. So when she returned the next week, the monsignor immediately asked, "Well, my dear, did you talk to Jesus this past week?"

"Yes, your holiness," the little girl replied.

"And when you talked to him this past week, did you remember to ask Jesus what I confessed to at my last confession?"

"Yes, your holiness, I did."

"Well," inquired the monsignor with barely concealed eagerness, "when you asked Jesus what I confessed to at my last confession, what did he answer?"

The little girl immediately responded, "Jesus said, 'I've forgotten.'"

You might want to think that the little girl was just a smart fabricator, but her answer was pure and perfect Christian theology. It is possible to acknowledge sin without contrition. But if we are genuinely repentant, then our sins are completely forgotten by God. It is as if they never existed. The slate is wiped completely clean. Every day can be a totally new one.

Then why is it that so many continue to berate themselves for their sinful past? The depressed can be experts at being displeasing to themselves, but they are not very serene about it as they bewail their shortcomings over and over again. "Your depression is connected to your insolence and refusal to praise," the Muslim Jalāl ad-Dīn ar-Rūmī (one of the greatest of the world's saints) said approximately eight hundred years ago in the most succinct and penetrating comment ever made about depression.[13] For when you scratch through the superficial pseudohumility of many depressed people, you are likely to discover a core of arrogance. This is why the church refers to continual breast-beating as the "sin of excessive scrupulosity." It is a perverted form of pride. Since God forgives them, the refusal of these people to forgive themselves reflects an often unconscious belief that they are higher than God. "I, not God, will be the judge," they insist.

The gift of appropriate guilt is also graceful because it is not only our single safeguard against our own evil but also one of the foundations of faith. Faith is knowledge. And knowledge is based on evidence. We have faith that the sun will rise tomorrow morning precisely because we have a great deal of evidence to support our expectation. From the evidence that the sun has risen every morning for billions of years, we are quite justified in concluding that it will rise tomorrow as well. But what is the evidence of God? It is not easy to see the evidence when we are lacking a personal sense of sin. If we feel we have it all together, that our knowledge is far-reaching and our wisdom is great, then we feel that we are competent enough to run the show. "Rich" in spirit, we may pay homage to our need for the sun and the rain, but, given these, who needs God? Believing that we have the puzzle all put together, God simply seems like an unnecessary piece to be discarded.

It is another matter, however, when we have been blessed with a sense of our own sin. Then our eyes are opened. They are opened

13. Jelaluddin Rumi, "Praising Manners," in *Night and Sleep.*

to the fact that what we think we know is but a minute fraction of what we need to know and what we think we know is probably wrong to begin with. We come to realize that we are pitifully ignorant creatures whose largest talent is the capacity for self-deception. It dawns on us that we couldn't survive except by supernatural protection. We are too small, too blind, too stupid, too selfish, too nasty even to begin to make it on our own. We make it only because we are parented, protected, watched over, and nurtured by an ever-present and ever-mindful God.

Then something else dawns on us. Aware, by virtue of our personal sense of sin, that we human beings are a sorry lot, we begin to wonder why it is that God sticks with us. Why doesn't He just chuck us? What causes Him to continue to watch over us? And then we understand. He loves us. He knows who we are. He knows all our little conceits and deceits, and still He loves us. And He continues to love us because, in His love, He forgives us—just as Jesus, who knew Peter would betray him, who knew Peter *did* betray him, still loved Peter and forgave him and made him the foundation of the church. So we arrive at that marvelous understanding that is the center of Christianity: that we continually sin and that we are continually forgiven. Like Peter, then, and like the songwriter, each of us will turn to this merciful God who continues to protect us and exclaim in humble wonder: "Lord, how You must love me!"

The dream of a utopia is as old as civilization. It has never been realized. If we nurture our sense of personal sin, however, someday we may yet fulfill our dream of a new Jerusalem, of heaven on earth. But until that time it will continue to be both appropriate and necessary to repetitively exclaim the Kyrie in desperate prayer:

Lord, have mercy
Christ, have mercy
Lord, have mercy.

THE LORD IS MY LIGHT AND MY SALVATION

(Based on Psalm 27)

T he Lord is my light and my salvation.
Of whom should I fear? I need not fear.
The Lord is the strength of my life.
I need not be afraid.
I need never be afraid.

Hear, O Lord my God, I'm calling.
Have mercy on me, please answer me.
Lord, it is You of whom my heart speaks.
My eyes are seeking You.
Hide not from me Lord.

One thing I ask, my God, and this I seek;
To spend my whole life in Your presence, Lord.
To ponder Your goodness, Lord, for all my days;
Be guided by You.
Please guide me Lord.

I believe that I shall see Your goodness, Lord.
In every passing day; in this moment, Lord.

To wait for my God with courage is my hope.
Give me Your courage, Lord.
Help me wait for You.

ANTIPHON
The Lord is my light and my salvation.

5 Faith

FAITH IS NOT EASY.

The preceding song "Lord, How You Must Love Me" is heavy, even depressed. It speaks of almost unredeemable weakness. The song for this meditation is powerful, resounding with the unshakable confidence that is faith. What is going on? Were they written by two different people? Or is the songwriter some kind of manic-depressive?

Neither is the case. These two songs are like the opposite sides of a coin; you cannot have one without the other. You cannot have genuine confidence without first having doubt. Perhaps the greatest sin of our sinful Christian Church has been its tendency through the ages to discourage doubt. I apologize on behalf of my miraculous yet crippled church to those who have suffered as a result of this sin, and I hope that what I write here will help to purify the institution that has kept alive the faith but could have done better. For how can we find answers if we do not ask questions? Like anything, doubt can be carried to sick and destructive extremes. But in ordinary amounts I believe it should be considered one of the Christian virtues. As I have said before, "The path to holiness lies through questioning everything."[14]

Just as we can only begin to know reality by traveling through the darkness of doubt, so it is that true self-confidence rests on self-knowledge, and realistic self-knowledge in turn can be achieved only through brutally honest self-questioning. Thus the one side of the coin must precede the other. The sense of personal sin must come first. Once you have developed it you can take to the road, swinging along the same kind of undefeatable marching rhythm with which Marilyn now sings. Thorns will not prick you. Bandits will not overtake you. Swing out and go forth.

But we don't swing out very easily. All of us run scared. At any given moment, more often than not, we are afraid of something. Will I be able to make the mortgage payment? Is the pain in my gut a cancer? Is the ache in my chest a heart attack? Does my husband have a girlfriend? Is my wife planning to leave me? Will my words seem weighty and wise? Will I get to the lecture on time? Will there be a bathroom there? What if she doesn't like me? Or even, as Prufrock asked, "Do I dare to eat a peach?"[15]

Many do not realize how frightened they are. They have been running scared for so long they have forgotten what it is like not to. And, of course, the macho types who proclaim that they are not

14. M. Scott Peck, *The Road Less Traveled* (New York: Simon and Schuster, 1978), p. 193.

15. T. S. Eliot, "The Love Song of J. Alfred Prufrock," in *The Complete Poems and Plays 1909–1950* (New York: Harcourt, Brace, 1952).

scared are the most frightened of all, because they even fear their own fear. Fear is such a constant companion in the background of our being we are usually neither aware of it nor able to imagine being without it.

"I need never be afraid," the songwriter sings. How can this be? Remember what was said in the preceding meditation on the sense of personal sin. First, it was pointed out that a sense of personal sin serves us as a watchdog against our own evil. Aware of our immense capacity to betray God, our neighbor, and ourselves, we can guard against such betrayals. Paradoxically, we need not be afraid of making mistakes when we are afraid of them. With a well-developed sense of personal sin, we do not have to fear ourselves.

Secondly, it was explained that the awareness of our own sinful weakness and inadequacy reveals to us the enormousness of God's grace. We realize that we are protected. Recall the lines of that great hymn "Amazing Grace":

> 'Twas grace that taught my heart to fear,
> And grace my fears relieved;
> How precious did that grace appear
> The hour I first believed!
>
> Through many dangers, toils and snares
> I have already come
> 'Tis grace that brought me safe thus far,
> And grace will lead me home.

By God's grace we are protected. We are safe. We will always be safe. We have been saved. Salvation has occurred. "I need never be afraid."

Does this means that Christians no longer run scared, that once they have seen the light they will never know fear again? No. It ought to mean that, but it doesn't. My heart still skips a beat when I see the police officer in the rearview mirror. I still worry whether my children will make it through college. All the old panicky questions still flit through my mind. Will the pipes freeze? Will the well run dry? Do I have enough insurance?

My faith is very small. Here I dare to write a book on Christian doctrine when in my day-to-day living I act as if I did not believe my very own words. Am I a hypocrite? I do not think so. I truly believe these things; I just don't believe them very well. Faith, you see, is a tricky business. There are a few Christians who somehow manage to achieve a solid, fearless faith. But for most of us, faith is a very shaky sort of thing. Indeed, the more faith we have the more we realize how terribly little we actually do possess.

Fifty yards below my house there is a large lake, and the sight of it through the trees causes me from time to time to contemplate the problem of walking on water. Not too many years ago I thought the business of walking on water utter nonsense. It couldn't be done. But the older I get the more miracles I see. Whenever Jesus talked of miracles he spoke of faith: "By your faith you have been healed," a phrase he repeated to those who were miraculously cured. The message, again and again, is that we can accomplish the seemingly impossible, if only we have enough faith. Could this be true? Could I walk down from my house and casually stride out across the lake? I have enough faith to ask the question but not enough to attempt the experiment. I am sure I would go glub-glub-glub if I did. My faith is all tentative and intellectual. I think that walking on water might be possible, but in my heart I am certain that I will immediately sink, coughing and sputtering. And so I would. But would I sink because sinking is inevitable, or would I sink by the weight of my doubt? Perhaps I would fail to walk on water precisely because my *real* faith is that I can't do it and will fail. Suppose, however, I believed that I really could succeed. . . .

Perhaps the notion of walking on water is a gimmick. And I do think Muhammad spoke wisely when he said, "Trust in God, but tie your camel first." Remember, "'Twas grace that taught my heart to fear" as well as "grace my fears relieved." But the issue is important. It is not a matter of speculation. Can a Christian businessman hold on to the faith that he will be protected if he tells the president of his company that a certain policy is unethical and that he cannot participate in its execution? Can a conscientious objector refuse to fight and know that it will turn out all right for him in the end? Will a woman who leaves the husband who beats her be assured of her safety? These are not gimmicky questions. During our lifetime each of us gets to confront such moral dilemmas. Sometimes they seem very dramatic. Sometimes they seem so ordinary we are hardly aware of them. Whether we dare to do the right thing or fearfully cop out is in large measure a reflection of our faith.

The problem with Christian faith is not that it is misplaced but simply that it is faith. We are like toddlers clutching fearfully at their mother's skirt. When she is in their sight and grasp, they are comfortable in the knowledge she is there. As soon as she departs from them, however, they panic for their safety. They have no faith that she is just in the next room and able to hear them, that she has not abandoned them, that her concern for them continues even when she is not there, and that she will return to them as soon as her presence is required. When we can actually see God and hold on to His robe, we have no need of faith. Faith comes into play only when God seems far away.

Like the good mother He (She?) is, God's concern for us continues even when we cannot see Him, and He will manifest Himself once again whenever our need becomes desperate enough. But we do not know this. And we are not comfortable with this state of affairs. We want our God back. So the songwriter sings to the God who is no longer near: "I'm calling You. Please answer me. I'm looking for You. Don't hide from me. I want to be with You all the time. I need Your guidance. Help me to wait for You until You come back." A ringing statement of faith, this song at the very same time is a prayer for faith.

Is Marilyn's faith so weak that she must pray for it? Of course; she is in the same boat as you and I.

But do not underestimate it. It is still faith. Atheists say there is no God because they cannot see Him. They will not acknowledge the reality of His concern unless they can clutch at His skirt every single moment of the day. They insist upon a God who requires no faith of them. They deny His existence simply because He is physically absent. But Marilyn has grown beyond the toddler stage. While she yearns for His presence when He seems absent, she is willing to stake her whole life on Him, and she will wait for Him in prayer as long as it takes.

Certainly we would like a God we could clutch on to every second. Whether that would be good for us, however, is another matter. How could we grow up at all if we were to stay clinging onto His robe? "It is to your advantage that I should go away from you," Jesus said to his disciples.[16] So also it is to our advantage that God should appear to depart from us. There is no other way we could grow in faith.

The time when God seriously appears to have abandoned us—when we even scream for Him and He does not seem to answer—has been called the "dark night of the soul." It is not an easy time. But all who have experienced it say the same thing: this time of weaning is a gift to us. In fact, in one dimension, faith is indeed a gift—something we cannot earn, a blessing that is given to us. Paradoxically in another dimension, there are ways in which we can develop this gift.

What are we to do when the dark night descends upon us— when we seem to deserve it least, when we seem to need the light most? The answer is clear. If God gives us the dark night to test and thereby increase our faith, then what we must do in the darkness is that which He asks of us: to believe. We can do no better than to sing or pray with our songwriter:

> I believe that I shall see Your goodness, Lord.
> In every passing day; in this moment, Lord.
> To wait for my God with courage is my hope.
> Give me Your courage, Lord.
> Help me wait for You.

16. John 16:7.

It is interesting that in this song of faith Marilyn speaks of both waiting and courage. I do not wait easily. In fact, I hate it. Recently I wrote a friend that I don't like to make snap decisions. A few days later I apologized to him for my lie. The truth is that I love to make snap decisions. The truth also is that my snap decisions are often wrong. So I have for some years been training myself to delay decisions when appropriate. It is hard work. Jogging is easier than fighting impatience. Waiting takes courage.

While I do not suggest that you try walking on water, the way to increase your faith is to risk acting as if you had it. "Fake it to make it" is a justifiably popular saying in Alcoholics Anonymous. So it is that I sometimes conduct on myself experiments in faith, and particularly the faith of waiting. Several years ago I attended a week-long course during the summer at Harvard University. Because I was lonely, I hoped that I would meet someone particularly interesting from among my several hundred fellow students. An obvious way to do this would have been to mingle at the cocktail party that was held every evening in the dormitory courtyard. But I don't like cocktail parties. So I said to myself, "I wonder what will happen if I just sit down with my drink in one corner of the courtyard and wait to see who will approach me?" The first evening no one did. But I resolved to continue to act as if I had the faith that the right person would. So on the second evening I took my solitary place once again in the corner. Within five minutes a man detached himself from the crowd and introduced himself to me. He was a brilliant and fascinating person, and we quickly became friends. During the rest of the week I had met enough of my fellow students to realize I had "picked" the cream of the crop.

A similar way to increase faith is to pray. Prayer is an act of faith. Even if we think that we no longer believe, we are in fact believing when we pray. Whether or not He seems to exist anymore, the very fact that we still call upon His name preserves for us the kernel of our faith in His existence through the dark night. There is no more elegant prayer than "I believe, Lord. Help my unbelief." The early Roman Christians had a proverb: "*Lex orandi, lex credendi,*" meaning that the rule of prayer precedes the rule of faith. Prayer begets faith and faith begets more faith. And if we keep praying through our dark night to the silent, invisible, seemingly absent God, it will eventually come to pass that He will return to us more real than ever before and more present than we ever dared imagine.

"The Lord is my light and my salvation. The Lord is the strength of my life. I need not be afraid," Marilyn sings. This is what Jesus taught us. "Be not anxious, oh ye of little faith," he said again and again. No message is repeated more often throughout the Gospels than this one: Don't worry. Behold the lilies of the field. . . . Don't worry. If His eye is on the sparrow. . . . Don't worry. If I fed the multitudes. . . . Jesus didn't mean there was nothing we should every worry about. He clearly instructed us to worry about the possible emptiness of our piety, about the beam in our own eye before we worry about the mote in our neighbor's. He wanted us to be worried about the health of our soul. His message is this: if we seriously concern ourselves with our spiritual life, the material things will be provided to us.

It is important to remember that even Jesus had his own dark night. Hanging from the cross, nails through his wrists, parched, all the muscles of his torso in spasm, barely able to breathe, with death almost upon him, God seemed absent even to Jesus. And Jesus cried out, "My God, my God, why have You forsaken me?" But it was still God he addressed. And soon thereafter, strange and glorious things began to happen. We need never be afraid.

But we still are. Faith does not come easily. I still run scared. However, as a result of my minuscule faith I run a little less scared than I used to. Thank God.

PRAYER FOR THE KINGDOM

(Based on Mark 12:28)

H ow shall we know the kingdom of heaven?
How shall we help it come to be?
Lord, please help us see, hear our voices,
Help us be the love You bear, the love You bear us.

Lord, teach us how to love each other,
Lord, how to live and how to die.
Lord, please help us see to be gift,
Yes, how to be the love You bear, the love You bear us.

REFRAIN
Love your God with all your heart,
With all of your mind,
And your neighbor as yourself.
Do these things
And you will know the love I bear, the love I bear you.

6 Worship

WORSHIP IS YET ANOTHER paradox of the religious life: it is simultaneously the greatest duty and the greatest pleasure of faith. Worship is the act of truly loving God. Believe in this brilliant Being, this magnificent "higher power," who not only created us but nurtures us with care and intelligence beyond our imagination, and obviously we are called to worship Him. Although grander, worship is not unlike the love between equals. If you truly love your spouse, then it is your duty to pay her or him attention; to praise your beloved for the beauty of his or her body, spirit, and behavior; to work in your beloved's behalf; to bring your beloved gifts. It is from this same attending and praising, working for a cause and gift-giving, that we human beings can derive our greatest pleasures and deepest sense of peace and purpose.

Just before the publication of my first book, *The Road Less Traveled*, I was vacationing at a small inn on the coast of Maine. Very pleased with myself, I made sure to drop hints of my forthcoming accomplishment. One of the other guests, a well-established trial lawyer, engaged me in conversation. In the course of our talk he inquired as to the nature of my new book. "It's a kind of integration of psychology and religion," I explained.

"Fine," he said. "But what does it say? What's the message?"

"That's a bit complicated," I replied. "It says a lot of things. I'm not sure you want to listen to me talk for an hour."

"You're right," he responded, beginning to pressure me as if I were on the witness stand. "All I want is a few sentences that get to the heart of the matter and tell me what the book really says."

"I don't think I can do that," I answered. "If I could have said it in a few sentences, I wouldn't have had to write a book."

"Nonsense," the man exclaimed. "We have an adage in the legal profession that anything worth saying can be said in two sentences or less—and if it can't be, then it's not worth listening to."

I regretted my pride of authorship that had led me into this predicament. "It certainly is possible you wouldn't find my book worth reading," I allowed, and then somehow I managed to steer the course of the conversation to a new direction.

The same sort of thing happened to Jesus in Jerusalem. Only, of course, Jesus handled himself infinitely more gracefully.

You can imagine it. A man came forth out of the crowd—you guessed it, a lawyer. "All these parables are very nice," he may have said, "but what is it you're really trying to say, Jesus? What's your message? I don't want a whole Sermon on the Mount. I just want a few succinct sentences. Come on, Jesus, give it to me straight and simple. What is it you're telling us we ought to do?"

And Jesus obliged him.

It was really no more than a single sentence. "Love the Lord, your God," Jesus answered him, "with all your heart and mind and soul, and your neighbor as yourself."[17]

That was all he said.

Jesus referred to this simple sentence as the two basic commandments and said they were "like unto each other." By this he meant, I believe, that each is a translation of the other. They are equivalents in different languages. If we are loving our neighbor as ourself, we are also loving God. And if we truly love God, we will truly love our neighbor. The love of our neighbor is the worship of God translated into action within this world.

The commandment to love our neighbor as ourself, also known to us as the Golden Rule, is so familiar that it needs little explanation. This is not because it is an easy commandment or because it is unimportant—it is neither easy nor unimportant—but only because it is familiar.

The other commandment, however, is downright strange in this secular age. "Love the Lord, your God, with all your heart and mind and soul." The words seem simple enough, but think upon them for a moment. There are a lot of people who do not believe in God at all. So, simple though the words may be, for nonbelievers these words are mere gibberish. Then there are others who hold on to a notion of God as some sort of abstract force or a kind of clock maker who once set the world in motion and long ago departed. These people cannot understand what Jesus meant either. Jesus said "your God," meaning a God who is in a direct,

17. Matthew 22:34–40.

personal living relationship with each and every member of his audience—even the lawyer. We cannot say "my" God to an abstract force or an Aristotelian prime mover.

But let me assume that for you God *is* a living reality, an active presence in your life—that He is *your* God. Then do you understand what Jesus meant when he said, "Love the Lord, your God, with all your heart and mind and soul"?

I am a stickler for honesty. When I sign a letter "Sincerely yours," it is because I am being sincere. When I end by saying "Best wishes," I mean just that: I do indeed wish my reader the best. Sometimes I sign off with "Love," and then I actually intend my reader to know that he or she is truly loved by me. Rarely I may conclude with "Much love," a message only to someone very dear, to someone particularly special in my heart. It has been many years—perhaps even since my teens, when my romantic passion was untempered by any realism—since I signed a letter "All my love," because I now know the truth to be that there is always some reservation in my heart or mind or soul. I cannot commit to total love. In all honesty, the most I can say is "I love you totally, as long as it doesn't interfere with my career," or "I love you totally, as long as things continue to go well between us." I don't know of any human being to whom I can say, "You have all my love" without that statement being in at least some small way a lie.

If you had written a letter to God last night, could you have told Him with complete honesty that He had *all* your love?

When Jesus said, "Love the Lord, your God, with all your heart and mind and soul," he was careful to cover all the bases. He does not leave you an out. Indeed, some versions of the Gospels even add "and with all your strength." There are no escape clauses. "All your heart and mind and soul" means all of you, without reservations; you must totally belong to Him. Jesus wasn't talking about a mature love as cautious adults usually think of it. He was talking about something much more akin to "first love," to that unbelievably bittersweet and innocent romantic love, when we could literally think of nothing other than our beloved, when we could honestly say "You have all my love." He didn't mean a restrained or balanced love. He meant worship. He meant that our love for God should be passionate—that we should relate to God with a kind of adolescent abandon that is required to make us wholly His.

Suppose we did throw caution to the wind and loved God in this way. Mightn't it mean vast changes and upheaval in our lives? Yes, it probably would mean that. It might mean that we would think much more about starvation in Africa and much less about our vacations in the Bahamas. In our passion it might even mean that we would follow Him into the slums and ghettos and prisons. God knows what might happen to us if we truly worshiped Him. It might be very painful. It might also be a way to live far more exciting and meaningful lives than we currently do.

It is perhaps a sign of how few of us are willing to take the risk of loving God with all our hearts and minds and souls that many may be surprised I have not yet mentioned attending church. Here I've been talking of private worship. For most Christians the very word *worship* may only refer to public worship conducted for an hour on Sunday mornings.

I do not mean to decry that one hour of public worship. To the contrary, it is currently my favorite hour—the highlight of the week. It's when I have the most fun.

Fun? Sunday morning in church, fun? As a child and teenager I occasionally went to church only because I had to, and I took the first opportunity to quit the egregious practice. Back then, that hour was three parts tedium and one part fear. The tedium was because I didn't have any idea yet about the passionate love of God, so it was a succession of meaningless minutes. My fear came from some dim sense of the holy. It seemed to me that the rituals of the Sunday-morning worship service—the liturgy—were holy and had better be done right. But no one ever told me how I was supposed to do them right. So the long moments of boredom were interspersed with brief ones of panic when I was certain I made some unholy liturgical goof. Things only began to get a little better when at age fourteen I summoned up my adolescent courage, opened my eyes during a period of prayer, and looked around at all those worshipers with their heads bowed piously. When God didn't strike me dead for this act of rebellion, I began to lose some of the fear, but by then I was pretty much out the door of the institutional church of my childhood.

Twenty-five years later, in the midst of beginning to fall head over heels in love with God (as I recounted in the Introduction), I took it into my head (or did He put it there?) to go to a convent for my first retreat. It involved me in five church services a day for two weeks! It was not just a matter that now, because I had truly begun to love God, public worship began to have meaning. Nor was it simply that, being immersed in liturgy, I learned the worship routine. It was also because, at least once a day, during those services, the nuns broke into joyous laughter. I shall always remember the moment in the midst of intercessions on the second day of my retreat when old Sister Gertrude suddenly prayed, "Thank you, God, for helping me to remember that I left the rice cooking on the stove," and dashed out of the chapel to keep it from burning.

It dawned on me then that liturgy is, among other things, play. And I also began to understand why Jesus called God "Abba" or "Daddy." We could play together! So goes one little chapter of how my Beloved led me back to church on Sunday mornings where I can now experience the fun as well as the power and the glory of public worship.

But much as I might like to on some days, I cannot spend all my waking hours in church. Inevitably, therefore, public worship is but a small and the least important part of what worship is all about. We are not called to be Sunday-morning Christians—to merely love the Lord, our God, between nine and ten in the morning one day a week. When Jesus said, "Love the Lord, your God, with all your heart and mind and soul," he meant every waking minute. He meant in everything we think and everything we do. He meant us to be loving God when we are brushing our teeth in the morning, when we're selling our wares, when we're riding the subway, when we're vacuuming the living room, when we're speaking with our children, cooking the asparagus, chewing on the chicken, and falling asleep into His arms at the end of the day He had given us.

When Jesus gave us his great commandments, he was not saying anything new. Actually, it was old hat. Many before him had said the same sort of thing, one way or another. What then was different about Jesus' teaching? His message was radical in that he preached about something called either the kingdom of God or the kingdom of heaven. The two great commandments of which we have been speaking may be the keys to that kingdom. What was new and different was that Jesus said that if we really could love the Lord, our God, with all our heart and mind and soul and our neighbor as ourselves, then we could enter this kingdom.

Where is this strange kingdom? Some have talked about it as a social utopia and suggested that if each and every one of us could wholeheartedly obey the two great commandments, then we could truly usher into this world a great society, and our planet Earth would become the kingdom. There is reason to believe that Jesus meant something like a great society. But we know that it was only a small part of what he meant—and likely the smaller part. What he also meant was that we can also enter the kingdom as individuals, each of us who is willing to pay the price. The kingdom is, among other things, a state of mind.

When we love the Lord, our God, with all our heart and mind and soul, then we don't do our "thing" anymore. We do God's "thing." The question is no longer "What do I want to do?"; it is "What do You want me to do, Lord?" As I have alluded, when we ask this question, God knows where we will be led. He may lead us into poverty, into imprisonment, and even into death. To love the Lord with all our heart and mind and soul is a very great risk. Why should we take it, then? What's in it for us? Where's the pleasure? What is this kingdom, this pearl, for which we should be willing to pay such a great price, even the price of our lives?

St. Thomas à Becket, in the words of T. S. Eliot, spoke of the kingdom in this way:

Reflect now, how our Lord Himself spoke of peace. He said to His disciples, "My peace I leave with you, my peace I give unto you." Did He mean peace as we think of it: The Kingdom of England at peace with its neighbors, the barons at peace with the King, the householder counting over his peaceful gains, the swept heart, his best wine for a friend at the table, his wife singing to the children? Those men His disciples knew no such things: they went forth to journey afar, to suffer by land and sea, to know torture, imprisonment, disappointment, to suffer death by martyrdom. What then did He mean? If you ask that, remember then that He said also, "Not as the world gives, give I unto you." So then, He gave to His disciples peace, but not peace as the world gives.[18]

David Williams echoed this refrain in his well-known hymn:

> They cast their nets in Galilee
> Just off the hills of brown;
> Such happy, simple fisher folk,
> Before the Lord came down.
>
> Contented, peaceful fishermen,
> Before they ever knew
> The peace of God that filled their hearts
> Brimful, and broke them too.
>
> Young John who trimmed the flapping sail,
> Homeless, in Patmos died.

18. T. S. Eliot, *Murder in the Cathedral* in *The Complete Poems and Plays 1909–1950* (New York: Harcourt, Brace, 1952), pp. 198–99.

Peter, who hauled the teeming net,
Head down was crucified.

The peace of God, it is no peace,
But strife closed in the sod.
Yet, brothers, pray for but one thing—
The marvelous peace of God.[19]

A minister, Gordon Powell, made it ever more clear for us:

When each one of us comes, as Paul did on the road to Damascus, to
say, "Lord, what wilt Thou have me to do?" then we will find how to
direct our fighting spirit not into some paltry and selfish battle, but into
real battle, the battle for the Kingdom of God. And the strange thing is
that when we get into that battle with all our heart and mind and soul,
then we discover His peace, the peace of God which passeth all understanding.[20]

A couple of years ago I actually did figure out what I was trying to say in a single sentence. Thinking over all the different
speeches and the sermons I deliver and the books I write, I won-
dered whether there was a single message underlying them. I realized there was. Whatever the topic, wherever I go, I am trying one
way or another in my own small way to help people to take God,
Christ, and themselves far more seriously than they do.

19. *The Hymnal of the Protestant Episcopal Church in the United States of America,* Hymn 437.

20. Gordon Powell, *Power Through Acceptance: The Secret Serenity* (Chappaqua,
NY: Christian Herald Books, 1977), p. 57.

Shortly after reaching this conclusion, I attended a small dinner party where one of the other guests, referring to a particular film producer, remarked, "He has left his mark on history." Without thinking, I suddenly blurted out, "We all leave our mark on history." The conversation stopped dead, as if I had said something grossly obscene.

Why does it make us so uneasy, this terrible importance to our lives which begins to dawn upon us as soon as we have some dim vision of the kingdom (and which most piercingly is made known to us by the love of God in Christ)? The responsibility frightens us. We would prefer to think of ourselves as ordinary, average, normal. We do not want the responsibility for history on our backs. But it's there whether we want it or not. The future of the kingdom in good part is up to us, and there are currently many indications that we may fail it. So it is, at this very moment, I am urging you toward genuine worship. Whether we believe it or not, each of us has been called to bring the kingdom into being—into our hearts and into the world.

COME TO ME

(Based on John 6:35–40, 7:37)

If there is anyone among you who is thirsty,
Then come to me, says your Lord.
  If there is anyone among you who is hungry,
  Then come to me, says your Lord.
  O come to me.
  For I am the bread of life, and I am the cup of salvation;
  And I long to give myself to you, and make you a new creation.
  So come to me, O come to me.

If there is anyone among you living in darkness,
Then come to me, says your Lord.
If there is anyone among you lost and lonely,
Then come to me, says your Lord.
O come to me.
For I am the rising sun, and I am the lover of your soul;
And I long to give myself to you, to love you and make you whole.
So come to me, O come to me.

Do you feel small and lonely, weary and heavy of heart?
Give me your hand and only believe me.
And let me come to you, O let me come to you.

7 Communion

COMMUNION, MORE FORMALLY called the Eucharist, is the central, common ritual of Christianity. "On the night before he was handed over to suffering and death," says one version of the story, "our Lord Jesus Christ took bread; and when he had given thanks, he broke it, and gave it to his disciples, and said, 'Take, eat: This is my body which is given for you. Do this for the remembrance of me.'"

"After supper he took the cup of wine; and when he had given thanks, he gave it to them, and said, 'Drink this, all of you: This is my Blood of the new Covenant, which is shed for you and for many for the forgiveness of sins. Whenever you drink it, do this for the remembrance of me.'"[21]

It is this ritual of eating bread—flesh—and drinking wine—blood—in remembrance of Jesus that more than anything else bonds Christians together. The word "company" means literally a group of two or more persons who break bread together. ITT and General Electric are not companies by true definition. But the

---

21. *The Book of Common Prayer* (Episcopal), Copyright © 1977, pp. 362–63.

church is. Regardless of its limitations, the church has remained for many centuries a group of people who, everyday and in every corner of the globe—in Africa and England, in North and South and Central America, in Spain, Greece, Russia, Singapore, and Australia—are breaking bread together in Jesus' name.

When we speak of someone having a nervous breakdown, we do not literally mean that the nerves break down. But we do mean that something snaps. Throughout my youth I had what could be called an "authority problem." But I refused to acknowledge it as a problem until one day at the beginning of my thirtieth year. I thought I had it all together—that I was OK. On that particular day, however, I was raked over the coals by my peers as well as by my professor at a case conference. An hour later I was issued a ticket for failing to stop my car at a stop sign. An hour after that I had a humiliating encounter with my commanding officer. My hands were shaking uncontrollably. And an hour after that, realizing I did not have it all together, my trembling fingers were "walking" through the yellow pages looking for an ad for a psychotherapist. It was not exactly a nervous breakdown. But it was a moment of breaking up my pride. It was also one of my finest moments. For although it was quite painful to ask for help, it was the beginning of a giant step toward greater health and self-understanding.

It is no accident that the central moment of this central liturgy of the Christian Church comes when the priest holds the bread over the high altar and breaks it—snap—proclaiming, "Christ, our passover, is sacrificed for us." And in celebrating the Eucharist we not only remember his sacrifice but also participate in it by expressing our own willingness to be sacrificed. Whether we know it or not, we are signifying a desire to be broken, and the breaking we mean is usually a breaking of our pride. It may seem a strange religion indeed in which the followers actually seek to be broken. But we know, paradoxically, that it is only through our breaking that we can grow toward health, wholeness, and holiness (all three words have the same Anglo-Saxon root).

Recently, I flew to San Antonio and sat next to a young man. Maybe he was a boy. He was nineteen, but looked a little older. It was the first time he had ever flown. It was also the first time he had ever been west of New York State. He was traveling to Lackland Air Force Base to begin his basic training as an airman. He would not get to his new barracks until midnight and would be awakened at five-thirty the next morning by some strange drill sergeant.

I asked him if he was nervous. He told me he wasn't nervous in the least.

An hour before San Antonio, in clear skies, he stumbled suddenly across my legs, spilling his ginger ale in my lap. Fortunately he made it to the lavatory just before he vomited.

Later, I told him that people's stomachs often get upset when they are encountering a whole lot of new things all at once. I told him I'd be vomiting too if I were leaving home for the first time, flying for the first time, and simultaneously entering an unknown and possibly harsh new world.

What I didn't tell him was that he might not have had to vomit if he could have acknowledged how scared he was. But maybe it was easier for him to vomit than to acknowledge fear. I did, however, offer a silent prayer that someday this young man would be able to admit his fear. I also prayed it would all go well for him. If I were entering basic training, I'd want people to pray for me.

If you are hungry, thirsty, if you are living in darkness, if you are lost or lonely, if you are small and lowly, weary and heavy of heart, Jesus says, "Come to me." If you are scared, he says, "Come to me."

The only problem is that if we are any of these things, we have to admit it first. We can't ask for help until we are able to say it: "I need help."

This past spring my wife and I were on vacation in Puerto Rico with our twelve-year-old son. Because he had never had the experience, we rented a boat with another family for a day of deep-sea fishing. It was exciting. Wahoos and tunas were striking our fishing lines one after the other, and everyone got a chance to catch one. But we soon learned that if we didn't reel our catch in quickly enough the sharks would get to it first. My catch turned out to be a big one. Toward the end of our battle I became very tired. I was still able to slowly turn the reel, but I grew afraid I couldn't get it in the boat in time. So I asked another man, a strongly built stranger, if he would take my hand on the reel in his and pull along with me. He did, and in no time the fish was landed.

I was very proud. Not because I'd caught a fish. I'd caught fish before, and anyone could have caught one that day. I was proud because I'd asked for help. I hadn't done that very often. Ten, maybe even just five years before, I would have been too proud to ask for help. I would have felt ashamed to do so in front of my son. I would have felt embarrassed by my lack of strength. And I would have lost the fish.

Communion is not something you do by yourself. For there to be a communion one body has to take hold of another body's hand. And that doesn't happen by accident. If a stranger's hand brushes against you in a crowd, you don't take it by accident, you move away. Unless you need that hand. Communion arises only out of mutual need.

Even Jesus has need. He isn't saying in this song, "Come to me if you need me." He's not a passive participant in the process. He's not telling us, "Come and take if you want; it doesn't matter one way or another, I couldn't care less." Quite the contrary, he says, "I long to give myself to you." He longs, yearns, aches with desire. He's practically begging you, "Please, I love you. Please come to me."

And if that sounds sexual to you, it's because it is. We're not accustomed to thinking of sexual things happening in the church, much less at the high and holy altar. But that's our fault. In most of our churches we've done something terrible to the celebration of the Eucharist—we've made it antiseptic. I don't know why, but I do know it's very sad. It's no longer a celebration. You can't celebrate anything antiseptically. It isn't even a communion anymore. For there to be a communion, there has to be some touching, a meeting of the flesh, an exchanging of the "juices."

I do not mean to imply that communion is simply a symbolic sexual orgy. A sexual orgy is just that; a sexual orgy and nothing more. The celebration of the Eucharist is a sexual ceremony of sorts, but it is many other things as well—none of them antiseptic—such as a cannibalistic ritual or a bloody sacrifice.

But the celebration is always mutual. It's strange. We think of ourselves as needing Jesus, but we don't think of Jesus needing us. We believe he sacrificed himself for us, but we give little thought to the fact that real communion requires us to also sacrifice ourselves for him.

I didn't always know these things. No one does. You don't just step out on the court for the first time in your life one day and play a perfect game of tennis. You watch, you practice, maybe you even take lessons, and slowly you learn more and more what the game is about. The first few times I took communion, I was very scared. Maybe not as scared as if I were entering basic training, but still scared. I'm always scared when I don't have much idea what I'm doing.

After one takes it a few times (unless you've had some good training, which I didn't), one gets a bit cavalier about communion. So you go up to the altar and take a little pasty wafer or crumb of bread and a sip of wine, and nothing much happens. No lightning outside of you, and none inside either. It just doesn't seem like a big deal. Even if you decide it's a pretty ritual, it's still something you can take or leave. You don't really need it, and certainly it doesn't need you.

A few years ago I was working with a Christian woman who had a strange terror of taking communion. After a certain amount of work on her pride, her terror almost magically disappeared. Shortly thereafter, during a session, she reported incidentally that she'd been to church the preceding Sunday. I asked her if she'd taken communion, and she told me she hadn't. "I thought you'd gotten over your fear of it," I stated, wondering.

"Oh, I have," she responded. "It doesn't bother me at all now."

"Then why didn't you take it Sunday?" I asked.

"I just didn't feel like it that morning," she responded.

"You didn't feel like it?" I repeated dumbly.

"Yes, I didn't feel like it."

So I lit into her. I figured it was time she began to learn what communion was really about. "When Jesus let himself be nailed to the cross that Friday morning, when he was strung up and his muscles began to go all into spasm, when he allowed his body to be broken for you," I asked, "do you think he *felt* like it?"

Sacrifice is not something we feel like. If it felt easy, fun, good, then it wouldn't be a sacrifice. By definition it requires some kind of breaking, some kind of suffering or submission or giving up; it requires that at least a little bit of blood be shed.

Actually, once we truly understand what we are doing, communion becomes a joyful experience. It does feel good. But before it can be that way, there must first be some sacrifice on our part. Usually it is a sacrifice of our pride. We must first admit that we need Jesus—that we are lonely and tired, hungry and thirsty, weak and living in darkness and frightened. Then we can come to Jesus. Then not only does Jesus say, "Come to me," but we say to Jesus, "Oh, let me come to you," and the barriers are broken, the sacrifice is mutual, and then there can be union.

So I asked my patient, "Did you ever think that maybe it isn't a question of whether you feel like taking communion or not? That whether or not you feel like it, maybe you need it? That maybe you are lost and lonely even when you don't feel lost and lonely? And that Jesus longs for you to come to him, and that by sitting smugly in your pew you are disappointing him? That maybe he needs you? That just maybe you have an obligation to sacrifice yourself for him as he sacrificed himself for you?"

Because they know they have an obligation and are humbly aware of their chronic need, many Christians make the celebration of the Eucharist a daily practice in their lives. Each day they may go far out of their way to attend Mass. They would not do so were they not hungry for Jesus, nor would they if they did not deeply desire to give themselves to him. I admire their faithfulness.

I myself attend Mass sporadically. The Eucharist celebration is a ritual. It is a wonderful ritual, and it is proper that God be worshiped not only through ritual, but also ritualistically. But it is also important to remember that communion need not be practiced only at the altar of a church. There need not even be bread and wine. Jesus will give himself to you whenever and wherever you come to him. He gives himself to me every morning during my first cup of coffee of the day. He gives himself to me in hotel rooms and on airplanes, and in the afternoon and the evening and in the middle of the night, whenever I ask him.

Nonetheless, the rules of communion are always the same. It must be mutual. It cannot occur unless I ask for it, and I cannot ask for it unless I am aware of my need for it, and I cannot be aware of my need unless I sacrifice my pride enough to realize my hunger and thirst, my ignorance and weakness and fear. Nor will it happen unless I surrender myself to Jesus as he surrenders himself to me.

But whenever I have the good fortune to be in a church where the blessed bread and wine are being served, I will thank God for you, Jesus, and I will never again pass you up.

IN QUEST OF WISDOM

(Based on Sirach 51:13–15, 18–22)

When I was young before I traveled on,
In my prayer I asked for wisdom.
Outside the holy place I prayed for her.
And to the last I'll be seeking her.
Yes, to the end of my days.

From her blossoming to her ripening,
My heart finds delight in her.
My foot pursuing the straight path she makes.
Bowing my ear I have received her.
She has helped me on my way.

To my core I've yearned to see her.
Directing my soul to her I've found her.
She's come to me in all my toiling.
A pure heart and life I gave for her.
She will be with me all my days.

Glory to Him who gives me Wisdom.
All of my life I've fought and now I've won.
Now that I've found her life has just begun.
Now she is mine and Lord, I have a tongue.
To sing Your praises evermore.

8 *Wisdom*

WISDOM IS FILLED WITH PARADOX. How many times in this book have I already mentioned paradox? In part, wisdom is the understanding of paradox. But, as if that were not enough, the acquisition of wisdom is itself paradoxical.

Marilyn sings of questing, yearning, praying, seeking for wisdom. Yet at the end of this song she exults: "Glory to Him who gives me Wisdom." Is there not something strange about this? Why should God get the credit? Clearly the songwriter, through questing, yearning, praying, seeking, worked hard for wisdom. Surely she earned it. Why should she thank God for it?

Fourteen centuries ago another hardworking religious professional, an Irish monk named Pelagius, taught his followers that they could earn their salvation by hard work. A thousand or so years ago, another group of Christians decided Pelagius was dead wrong—that salvation could not be earned, that it was a pure gift from God arising out of His grace. So they stopped working for their salvation. They called themselves Quietists, because they just sat around quietly waiting for that grace to happen.

Today we consider both Pelagianism and Quietism to be heresies. And well we should. For heresy usually arises when one refuses to see the whole reality and hence lives and teaches a one-sided life. For reality is usually paradoxical, and the truth about salvation is this: it is the product of a mysterious paradoxical mixture of individual effort and the unearned gift of God's grace. Salvation is an interaction—a dance between God and His beloved creature. God offers His hand. His beloved rises up to take it. God leads, the beloved follows, sometimes smoothly, sometimes stumbling and effortfully. The waltz has started. And once started, it goes on and on.

It is no accident that the paradox of wisdom immediately led me to speak of the paradox of salvation. For they are one and the same thing. The end of all wisdom is to know God and, conversely, to dance in His arms is salvation precisely because it is from that dance that wisdom is born.

Carl Sandburg wrote the following poem entitled "Limited":

I am riding on a limited express, one of the crack trains of
    the nation.
Hurtling across the prairie into blue haze and dark air go
    fifteen all-steel coaches holding a thousand people.
(All coaches shall be scrap and rust and all the men and
    women laughing in the diners and sleepers shall pass
    to ashes.)
I ask a man in the smoker where he is going and he
    answers: "Omaha."[22]

22. In *Modern American Poetry*, edited by Louis Untermeyer (New York: Harcourt, Brace, 1926), p. 240.

Marilyn begins her song on wisdom by singing, "When I was young before I traveled on, in my prayer I asked for wisdom." In other words, before she began her adult journey she sat down— or kneeled down—and gave a lot of thought to just where she wanted to go, unlike the man in the smoker in Sandburg's poem who was thoughtlessly hurtling through life from one empty destination to another. Had that man been more like Marilyn—had his awareness not been so limited—when asked where he was going, he might have replied, "I am going to meet my death in the fear and hope of glory." Instead the poor fellow could only answer, "Omaha."

I was raised in a time and place where superficialities were considered to be of the utmost importance. What prep school one attended was a crucial question. Whether the fork went on the left or the right was a burning issue. "Clothes make the man," my parents used to tell me. Disillusionment was bound (for me at least) to follow. Sooner or later, it was inevitable that I would run across a well-dressed idiot.

So at a relatively early age, like Marilyn, "before I traveled on," I developed a habit of looking beneath the surface. It is a habit that has stood me in good stead. "Forget the superficialities," I said to myself. "What is it that really matters? What is it that is most important about life?"

The most immediate answer was "Death." I am going to die. We are all going to die. It seemed to me a rather important fact of my existence, of anyone's existence here on earth—that it is temporary. Like the title of Sandburg's poem, it is limited. We are hurtling through space and time, and we shall soon all turn to dust and ashes.

For the more superficial person, the reality of death produces a sense of meaninglessness. Since we will be chopped down by the grim reaper like so much straw, what possible meaning could there be to our paltry human existence? But as I began to struggle with this question, with the mystery of my death, I discovered the opposite: death does not take away the meaning of our lives, it gives meaning to our lives.

Realizing I did not have all the time in the world, I began to wonder, "How do I want to use my life? Where is it I want to go with my limited time? What is the most proper course to follow?" And it was with these questions that I began my own personal quest for wisdom.

They are religious questions. They are neither asked nor answered in textbooks of physics; not even in textbooks of psychiatry. Questions of human meaning are dealt with only in religious books—the Bible, the Koran, the Upanishads, for example—and in religious places. So like the songwriter, it was "outside the holy place I prayed" for the answers.

Of course, many religious people, Christian and non-Christian, have no taste for struggling with Mystery—including the mystery of their death—any more than atheists do. They would like to exclude it from their awareness and thereby limit their pain and uncertainty, like the man in the smoker. Many religious people may simply parrot the answers written on the walls of the holy places. But theirs is a secondhand, hand-me-down religion; and while such religions, like secondhand clothes, may help to keep us warm, they are also just trappings. A deeply meaningful personal religion always requires a personal struggle with the mystery of death, among other mysteries. No one else can struggle for you, which may be the message behind the famous saying that "God has no grandchildren." We cannot relate to God simply through our parents' faith.

Thus, although we have been vastly helped by the words of holy books and the support of our sisters and brothers, our search for meaning, for wisdom, is a solitary journey on a certain level. On another level, our search has not been solitary at all, however, because God has been with us all along, assisting, guiding, even initiating the search. So, despite all her personal efforts, Marilyn still sings, "Glory to Him who gives me Wisdom."

You see, there is an unanswered, unanswerable question. What makes believers different from the man in the smoker? Where did the songwriter get the wisdom to look for wisdom in the first place? She would reply, "It is nothing that I earned. I cannot explain it, beyond saying that it was simply given to me by God's pure grace."

A year before she died, my mother was chatting at a cocktail party with a younger woman who knew of my work and who remarked, "You must be very proud of your son." With the tart wisdom sometimes typical of the elderly, my mother responded, "No, not particularly." The younger woman looked perplexed. "I had nothing to do with it, really," my mother explained. "It's his mind, you see. It's a gift."

While my mother deserved more credit than she took, she was quite right, I believe, when she said it was a gift, for which I can take no credit whatsoever. Where she was wrong, perhaps, was in identifying the gift with my mind. My IQ is not in the least impressive. Actually, I believe I have been given several gifts. The preeminent one is a thirst for meaning. I do not know where this thirst came from. It was simply with me. I have never wanted to undertake a meaningless journey. And, one way or another, all of my journeys have been quests for further meaning, thank God. It is a gift.

Eighteen years ago I had the opportunity to participate with a dozen other psychiatrists and mental health professionals in a marathon "encounter" group. After roughly fifteen hours of intensive work, we became what I call a "true" group—a genuine community. There was much laughter and good spirit among us, as we learned how to quickly focus on and resolve divisive issues. Along about the thirty-hour mark we observed that notes of anger and distrust had slipped back into our interrelationship. We stopped and asked why this was happening. Shortly we realized that the twelve of us were divided into two equal-sized camps. My group of six identified the other six as marching under the Sears and Roebuck banner. They, the materialists, in turn identified us as marching under the banner of the Holy Grail; so my camp came to be known as the Grailers.

Being an efficient group, we quickly recognized that in the limited time left to us, the Sears and Roebuck camp would not be able to help us Grailers come to our senses so as to stop chasing after some spiritual will-o'-the-wisp. Similarly, we Grailers accepted the fact that we would be unable in the few remaining hours to convert the Sears and Roebuck camp from their crass materialism. So we agreed to disagree, set our differences aside, and successfully got on with our work.

The theologian Michael Novak distinguished between two types of mentality: the secular consciousness and the sacred consciousness.[23] An individual with a secular consciousness considers himself or herself to be the center of the universe. Such individuals are often very sophisticated. They realize that every other individual considers himself or herself to be the center of the universe. They also realize that they are but single individuals among five billion of us human beings scratching out an existence on the surface of a small planet, circling a medium-sized star among millions of stars in but one of countless galaxies. So even though an individual with secular consciousness considers himself or herself to be the center of things, he or she is often afflicted with a sense of meaninglessness.

The situation is exactly the opposite for those with a sacred consciousness. Here the individual does not consider himself or herself to be the center of the universe at all; the center of the universe is God. Rather than suffer from a sense of meaninglessness that results from the belief in the centrality of the ego, however, individuals blessed with the sacred consciousness find their lives filled with meaning by virtue of their relationship to the true center. God gives them meaning. So, egoless in one way, they paradoxically know themselves to be of great importance in the scheme of things—an importance derived from God.

The sacred consciousness is wisdom. It is salvation. The quest for wisdom is the quest for transformation—the conversion of secular consciousness into—and ever deeper into—the sacred consciousness.

23. Michael Novak, *Ascent of the Mountain, Flight of the Dove*, Rev. ed. (New York: Harper & Row, 1978).

Repeatedly, the songwriter refers to wisdom as "she." This is no arbitrary feminism. Nor is it simply that God is feminine as well as masculine. It is no accident, I think, that more women than men seek out psychotherapy, any more than it is an accident that one is more likely to find more women than men worshiping in our churches. Wisdom requires the fertilizer of the intellect for its fullest flowering. But its seed is initially planted in the heart. It is primarily an intuitive phenomenon. Whatever the final results of right brain/left brain research may prove—whether male/female differences are more sociological than biological—there does seem to be a feminine quality to the gift of wisdom, as well as a feminine receptivity to that gift. I myself think of the Holy Spirit as predominantly feminine.

Be that as it may, wisdom is still a gift mysteriously given. I do not think we shall ever fully know why one person will have a clear and compelling vision of the kingdom, while another will be utterly and apparently permanently blind to it. It was something that Jesus himself said he did not understand. In his conversation with Nicodemus about being born again, he noted, "The wind blows here and the wind blows there, and no one knows on whom this new life from heaven will next be bestowed."[24]

Perhaps in the scheme of things we Grailers need the Sears and Roebuck folk. But we are the fortunate ones. We know that we have been given a gift they have not, which is why we can so often seem obnoxious in our eagerness to impart the gift to them. It is natural that this eagerness should be interpreted as a kind of moral smugness and self-righteous sense of superiority, even

24. John 3:8.

when it is not. And unfortunately, it often is. We must try to remember that we can only truly impart the gift with humility.

Insofar as we can impart it at all. As a professional psychotherapist, I have come to be profoundly impressed by the limitations of my profession. At best I can only facilitate the transmission of wisdom. In truth, the gift of wisdom is not mine to give. It is God's. Glory to Him who gives us Wisdom.

A NEW SONG

(Based on Matthew 7:7)

Wisdom is a spirit, a friend to man.
Listen all you people, hear and understand.
The Word is God's gift to you,
To bring you light,
To give you strength and courage to fight the good fight.

Worship now in spirit. You will come to know
All the Father has to give to make His Spirit grow.
We are called to freedom.
We are called to be
Living words of truth to give the Truth that makes us free.

REFRAIN
And I say:
Ask and you will receive.
Seek and you will find.
Knock and it will be opened to you.
And I say:
The Lord will give you His mind,
The Lord will show you the way.
The Lord will make you His light.

9 *The Holy Spirit*

THE HOLY SPIRIT or "Holy Ghost" used to amuse me as a school-age child. Everyone (in my twentieth-century upper-middle-class, secular American culture) knew that ghosts were not real. The notion of spirits was believable—as far as I was concerned—only by Indians or other kinds of primitive tribes living in the jungle. I knew that some people called "Catholics" occasionally talked about not only a ghost or spirit, but one that was "holy." I therefore assumed they were either some primitive religious sect in our own country or somehow not being serious. How could they be serious?

But as the Apostle Paul said in that famous passage familiar even to unbelievers: "When I was a child, I spoke as a child, I understood as a child, I thought as a child; but when I became a man, I put away childish things; now I know in part, but then shall I know even as also I am known."[25] My schooling is hardly complete. It is a theme of my education, however, that many of the idols of my childhood have been toppled and, conversely, much of what I once thought superstition I now proclaim as truth. So here I

25. 1 Corinthians 13:11–12.

am, forty years later, writing meditations to the songs of a Catholic nun, and this one in particular to a song about the Holy Spirit. It is the second wisdom song—perhaps much like a college class called Wisdom 2, an advanced-level course for which the first song, "In Quest of Wisdom," is a prerequisite to explore the mystery in greater depth and detail.

So let me begin where I left off at the end of the first course, saying: "As a professional psychotherapist, I have come to be profoundly impressed by the limitations of my profession. At best I can only facilitate the transmission of wisdom. In truth, the gift of wisdom is not mine to give. It is God's. Glory to Him who gives us Wisdom."

Perhaps the major means of my teaching is language. I am particularly impressed—as probably any serious writer is—by the inadequacy of words. And all the more so in matters such as these. No one put it better than the American poet John Hall Wheelock, in the last lines of "Unison," written at the end of his long and wise life:

> And whosoever in his heart has heard
> That music, all his life shall toil to say
> The passion of it. But there is no word—
> No words are made for it. There is no way.[26]

---

26. John Hall Wheelock, "Unison," in *This Blessed Earth: New and Selected Poems 1927–1977* (New York: Scribner's, 1978).

So it is that when God decided we needed a new song—a new teaching—He spoke to us not in words alone, but with His very Being. In Christ, God came down "to live and die as one of us." If Jesus had spoken to us in words alone, only then to retire on his pension plan, his teaching—wise beyond belief—would never have touched us. It has barely begun to sink in, but it would not have taken root at all if his message was just presented in words. It lives because he dies for us, because he taught us not solely with proverbs and parables, but with his body and blood as well. To put it crassly, he "put his money where his mouth was." Or, as some would say, "He walked his talk." It is for this reason that Christ is not words, but the Word—God's teaching, God's gift to us, all wrapped up in the single, whole, living/dying, human/ divine, suffering, penetratingly real package of His flesh.

If God made His teaching incarnate, then what is this about wisdom being a spirit? It is not an easy question to answer—in words. We humans have difficulty thinking about spirit, much less talking about it. The best I can do is use an inept analogy. It is as if Christ—the message, the Word—is not only given to us in the historical Gospels, but also being actively beamed to us by celestial radio. God knows it is not enough for us thick-headed humans to give us His wisdom in history; He must continue to give it to us in the present moment, minute by minute by minute. To get through to us He must continually bombard us by a kind of airwave that we have come to label the Holy Spirit. The meta-physics of this transmission are mysterious, except that the spirit seems to operate through our unconscious mind. God's wisdom bubbles up into our awareness out of the depths. Because in the depths of our consciousness we are, by spirit, connected with our Creator.

Why are so many utterly unaware of this connection, and so many others only dimly aware? The reasons are numerous. We live in a materialist culture in which the denial of spirit is sanctioned. Instead of employing our science to look more deeply for God, we use it to declare Him out of bounds. In some universities it is actually fashionable to teach that what cannot be measured does not exist. The arrogance of it is extraordinary. We presume that our little rules and clocks can encompass Reality. Rather than recognize our limitations, we strive to limit the world. Unable to cut it down to our own size, we deny the immeasurable. In some ways our arrogance masks our fear. We are afraid of the immeasurable Spirit, the power of love beyond all comprehension. We want to be in control of life; God forbid that life should be in control of us.

But even if we dare to acknowledge spirit, our minds are often so cluttered with petty self-centered preoccupations, so filled with self-made noise, that we cannot possibly hear God speaking to us in spirit. And even if we can quiet ourselves sufficiently to listen, we still may not truly hear because we do not like what God has to say. The voice of the Holy Spirit can often demand from us what we do not want to give; in fact, Her voice often seems a little bit crazy.

I recently met a woman in her late thirties who had traveled remarkably far on the spiritual journey, but was still deeply engaged in confronting her general fearfulness and lack of faith. She was accustomed to jogging every evening (some of my best friends are runners). One morning a week before our meeting, as she was putting on her lipstick just before going out the door to work, the "still, small voice" inside her said, "Go running."

She shook her head, as if to shake away the voice, and continued with her makeup. But the voice came back. "Go running," it said again.

"That's ridiculous," she replied, half to herself, half to the voice. "I don't go running in the morning. Besides, I'm on my way to work."

"Go running *now*," the voice insisted.

My friend had learned to take such persistent voices seriously. As she thought about it she realized it made no real difference whether she got to her office at ten that morning instead of nine. So, in obedience, she got all undressed again and into her jogging outfit.

After she had run a mile and a half in the park, she was feeling most awkward. "I don't know what I'm doing out here," she thought. "I'm not enjoying it. I don't feel comfortable running in the morning. I ought to go home right now."

At that point the voice spoke again. "Close your eyes," it commanded.

"That's crazy," she countered. "You don't close your eyes when you're running."

"Close them anyway," the voice responded.

So once again in obedience, she closed her eyes. After two strides she opened them in panic. But she was still on the path, and no one was in her way.

"Close them again," the voice ordered.

She did, with the same results. "Now do it again," the voice repeated. This time she made it four strides before her fear compelled her to look to see if she was still on the path and in no danger.

"That's pretty good," the voice commented. "Now keep on closing them."

Eventually she was able to make it up to twenty strides with her eyes closed, never running off the path or into trouble. At which point the voice said, "That's enough for today. You can go home now."

As she finished telling me this story, my new friend's eyes filled with tears. "To think," she exclaimed with joy, "that the Creator of the whole universe would take the time to go running with me!"

It is no accident that this woman listened to the voice and obeyed. I said she traveled far on her journey. Like the songwriter, she had spent much time asking for wisdom, seeking and praying for it "outside the holy place." As both Jesus promised and Marilyn sings: "Ask and you will receive. Seek and you will find. Knock and it will be opened to you."

My running friend's "voice" did not come to her when she was in prayer or meditation; it came when she was putting on her lipstick. The Holy Spirit is like that. She often speaks to us when we least expect it. But She can be heard and obeyed only when Her voice falls upon a prepared soul. And while moments of great revelation may not occur at such times, to have a fully prepared soul one must spend time in prayer and meditation.

Not long ago I was leading a small intensive workshop in conjunction with a minister who was a masterful conductor of what are called "guided meditations." At the very beginning of the workshop he asked us to relax and close our eyes, and then he gently led us as follows: "Imagine you are in your bedroom at night in the dark. But you notice a light under the closet door. You are curious. You get up, open the door, and find that the light is coming from behind a trapdoor on the closet floor. You open the trapdoor and discover a circular staircase descending into the most exquisite light. Go down that staircase and you are in an enormous light-filled room. It feels like a cathedral. Along the walls are marvelous artifacts from ancient Greece and Rome, from Mexico and Peru and Africa, from all great cultures since the beginning of time. Walk down that long, wonderful room, and toward the end there is a huge altar. And then you notice that there is a hooded figure seated silently before the altar praying. Although you cannot see the face, you sense this to be a person of great holiness. After a while you feel compelled to talk to this extraordinary, wise personage. Imagine now what she or he says to you, and the glorious expression on his or her shining face."

After this guided meditation, the group was asked who had thought that the holy figure was inside of them—a part of them-selves—and who had thought of this personage as an external and other being. Half thought one way and half the other. Only one in ten thought of the figure both ways. That small minority was theologically correct. God is paradoxically both inside of us in that still, small voice and outside of us in all His magnificent glory.

When I pray, it is to the external God that I speak. When I meditate, it is to the God within myself that I listen. In either case

I am in relationship with God, and it is out of the ground of that relationship that wisdom flows. The goal is to stay continually in that relationship.

In his guided meditations, the minister at the same workshop kept directing us participants to "find our center." The concept of "center" and "centering" is both fashionable and useful these days. People at the workshop often talked about where the "center" was located. Some said it was in their solar plexus; others in their abdomen. They had not, I think, completely evolved from secular consciousness into sacred consciousness. When asked where my center was, by the grace of God I was able to respond, "In my relationship to Him."

I have addressed how the Holy Spirit connects us to God and how we can center ourselves in relation to God. To take this connection, this relationship, seriously and reverently is what the songwriter means when she lovingly commands us, "Worship now in spirit."

She goes on to say that if we do this, we will "come to know all the Father has to give." Do you realize the glory of what she is telling you? Do you realize how incredibly wonderful it is? Almost beyond belief! Through this connection, through this worshipful relation, "the Lord will give you His mind." The very mind of God can be yours!

But only in the humility of true worship. While the Holy Spirit may work through us, She is not of us. We are not talking about self-worship; we are talking of its opposite: the forgetting of self, the emptying of self, the submission of self.

"We are called to freedom," Marilyn sings in this meditation. God wants us to be free. He is yearning for us to be free. He will do anything to set us free. But freedom is a paradox. On the one hand, free will is the essence of humanness. It even takes precedence over God's will for us, just as it takes precedence (and I speak here with the authority of a lengthy career in psychiatry) over healing. However, as I have written before:

We can be free to choose without shibboleths or conditioning. On the other hand, we cannot choose freedom. There are only two states of being: submission to God and goodness, or else the refusal to submit to anything beyond one's own will—which refusal automatically enslaves one to the forces of evil. We must ultimately belong to God or the devil. . . . I suppose the only true state of freedom is to stand exactly halfway between God and the devil, uncommitted either to goodness or to utter selfishness. But that freedom is to be torn apart. It is intolerable. . . . We must choose. One enslavement or the other.[27]

In the matter of this call to freedom, T. S. Eliot spoke of those who have responded fully to the call: the saints. The true saint, he wrote, "is he who has become the instrument of God, who has lost his will in the will of God, not lost it but found it, for he had found freedom in submission to God."[28] In other words, the connection, the relationship to God, can become so fully established that the individual no longer exists as an individual, and might even say, as did Jesus, "I and my Father are One."

27. M. Scott Peck, *People of the Lie* (New York: Simon and Schuster, 1983), pp. 83–84.

28. T. S. Eliot, *The Complete Poems and Plays, 1909–1950* (New York: Harcourt, Brace, 1952), p. 199.

IT IS HE

(Based on Galatians 2:19–20; 3:13, 25–29; 4:4–7; 5:1)

I live now not with my own life
But with Jesus the life living in me.
Here in this flesh I live in faith,
Faith in the life of Christ Jesus my Lord.

God sent His Son born to die;
To redeem us and make us His very own.
Place His Son within our hearts.
Now sons and daughters of His, His glory our own.

Cursed the man who dies on a tree.
This was the death Christ Jesus suffered for me.
Here and now we're chosen to be;
To reveal His grace that all then may see.

REFRAIN
Son of God who loves me and gives Himself for me,
It is He I give you.
It is He.
His life's blood has made you free.

10 *Sacrifice*

SACRIFICE, LIKE GUILT and sin, is not a popular idea these days, even among some who think of themselves as spiritual seekers.

One such spiritual seeker, a man in his middle forties, came to see me a few years ago to ask for spiritual direction. He was, he informed me, at a crossroads in his life. About to leave his job, he was free to do anything, to go anywhere. He had in mind the possibility of a Zen Buddhist monastery in Vermont, but was also thinking about joining a New Age commune in California. On the other hand, there was a sort of voice in the back of his head suggesting that he should turn his attention to Christianity, which he had not done since he escaped from church when he entered college. "Which way do you think I should go?" he asked.

"Heavens," I responded, "I can't begin to have an answer for such a question without knowing much more about you. Tell me all about yourself."

In the course of the next hour, he let me know that he had been married twice. He had two children by his first marriage, whom he had not seen for eleven years, and one by his second, whom he had not seen for six. I asked him why he had not seen his own children for so long. "There was a lot of stress and anger at the time of each divorce," he answered. "It seemed to me it would be less of a hassle for all concerned if I just got out of the picture and stayed out. Anyway, that's all in the past. The question I want you to help me with is what to do now. Which way should I turn?"

"Perhaps I don't know," I replied. "Perhaps all I can do for you is to speak of my own turnings.

"You probably don't know this," I continued, "but recently, at the age of forty-three, I was baptized as a Christian. Obviously my baptism represented a Christian commitment. And just as obviously, I would not have made that commitment, after all these years and after some slight familiarity with the other religions of the world, if I thought that Christianity was a second-best religion or even if I thought one religion had as much to offer me as another.

"At the core of all great religions there is a central notion, and in regard to such core ideas the other religions may speak more eloquently than Christianity. So, at the core of Buddhism is the notion of attachment and nonattachment. When I am dealing with patients who have problems with jealousy, possessiveness, addiction, or excessive bonding, I may well talk to them in Buddhist rather than Christian language. Similarly, from the little I know of Islam, it is much better at encouraging the remembering of God than is Christianity. But at the center of Christianity is the notion of sacrifice, and if you will pardon the pun, I have come to conclude that that notion is *crucial*. It does not mean, necessarily, that you should go about getting yourself crucified at every turn. But what it does mean, at the very least, is that whenever there is a decision to be made, which may be many times a day, an alternative should not be discarded simply because it is sacrificial."

The man looked at me dumbly. "What did you say?"

I repeated my last sentence: "What being a Christian means, at the very least, is that whenever there is a decision to be made, an alternative should not be discarded simply because it is sacrificial."

I know that this spiritual seeker intellectually understood my definition. Since he decided not to return to see me, I am uncertain whether it helped him to choose his best path. I hope so. But it is not an easy definition to swallow. The fact that Christian doctrine may be true does not necessarily make it palatable.

Still, when we tend to think of sacrifice as a gloomy sort of business, we ignore the reality that it is ultimately liberation. A personal example may make my point. A few years ago, while speaking in Jackson, Mississippi, for the first time, I was put up by a lovely family I'd not known before. I arrived at night, and they asked me what I liked for breakfast. I told them simply lots of black coffee and, if they really wanted to gild the lily, a glass of orange juice. In turn I inquired what time they ate and set my alarm accordingly.

About five minutes before my alarm went off the next morning, there was a knock on my bedroom door. I mumbled I was awake, and in walked my host, bearing a tray with a mug of hot steaming coffee, smelling rich of Mississippi chicory, and a large glass of fresh orange juice. Ten years previously, when I still prided myself on how much easier I found it to give than receive, I would have jumped out of bed saying, "Oh, no, Joe, you don't have to do that." Or, if I had not wanted to make a scene, I would awkwardly, uncomfortably, have accepted this service, but I would have made sure to set my alarm fifteen minutes earlier the next morning so as not to be waited upon. Because through psychotherapy and other help I had made the "great" sacrifice of pride involved, however, this was not how I behaved. Having made some progress in the battle against my pseudoindependence, I can now enjoy breakfast in bed with relaxed gratitude whenever I have the good fortune to be so served.

I do not mean to imply that the process of sacrifice is painless. Even if it is just our pride —usually it is only our pride —that we are sacrificing, it still hurts. But I do mean to imply that appropriate sacrifice ultimately reaps us rewards that far outweigh any pain involved.

After a few sessions I no longer allow patients or students to use the word "unselfish." I tell them that I am a totally selfish human being. When I water my flowers I do not say to them, "Oh, look, flowers, at what I am doing for you; you should be grateful to me." No, I am doing it for myself, because I like pretty flowers. As far as I am concerned, there is only the distinction between smart selfishness and stupid selfishness.

You may look at monks and nuns and, thinking of all their sacrifices and self-denials—sex, marriage, children, personal property—you may say, "Surely, they are unselfish." But I tell you that they are as selfishly motivated as any other human being. You see, they want joy. That's what they're after. Actually, it is what we are all after. It's just that they are smarter about it than most of us. They know that the only true path to joy is through sacrifice.

Yes, it would have hurt a little bit for that man who came to see me to stick around amid all that stress and "hassle" so as to try and be a real father to his children. Some sacrifice would have been required on his part. But, my God, think of the rewards he could have reaped! Even as a mediocre father, I have learned more from my children and grown more as a result than from any other source.[29] Although this seeker apparently made no effort to sacrifice for his children, I can feel deep sorrow not only for them but also for him, a poor man who came to see me about his spiritual journey when all along he had deprived himself of any real opportunity for spiritual travel. If only he had learned the meaning of Jesus' words: "And he that taketh not his cross and followeth after me is not worthy of me. He that findeth his life shall lose it: and he that loseth his life for my sake shall find it. He that receiveth you receiveth me, and he that receiveth me receiveth him that sent me. . . . And whosoever shall give to drink unto one of these little ones a cup of cold water only in the name of a disciple, verily I say unto you, he shall in no wise lose his reward."[30]

This song, "It Is He," like the sacrifice of which it sings, is both the climax and the turning point.

In *The Road Less Traveled,* I wrote that the goal of evolution is for human beings to "become God." Nothing I have written has given readers so much theological indigestion. And for good reason. The notion of "becoming God" can only be safely swallowed

---

29. For the best book on the subject of learning from your children, I suggest you read Polly Berrien Berends, *Whole Child, Whole Parent: A Spiritual and Practical Guide to Parenthood,* Rev. ed. (New York: Harper & Row, 1983).

30. Matthew 10:38–42.

in conjunction with the antacid of kenosis—the companion notion of self-emptying.

Satan fell like lightning from heaven when he tried to be God. A creature, he rebelled against the will of his own Creator. If we think of ourselves becoming God, are we not guilty of the same extraordinary arrogance? And will we not fall like Satan?

Or like Icarus? Fashioning himself wings of wax and feathers, Icarus attempted the reach the sun—godhead—under his own steam. But as he barely began to approach his destination, the heat melted the wax and he plummeted to his destruction.

Yes, we creatures *cannot* become God by ourselves. In fact, we can only become God *without* our selves.

That human beings not only can but should strive to become God is actually common doctrine for many Christians—those belonging to the orthodox churches, where it is known as "the deification of man."[31] But it is acceptable doctrine only when coupled with the realization that we cannot become God except by giving up our selves. We must first mostly bump our selves off.

The image often used in Christianity is that of the empty vessel. It is our task to empty ourselves of self—of our preoccupations with self, our pretensions and self-centered ambitions. Only when we are thus emptied can we then be filled by God.[32]

---

31. This is one piece of sexist language I would certainly like to change if I could to "the deification of humans."

32. Although usually thought to be a secular endeavor, psychotherapy is a part—often an essential part—of this self-emptying process. Among the things we must empty ourselves of are all the unnecessary psychological ways in which we protect ourselves. It is the purpose of psychotherapy to liberate patients from these inefficient and burdensome and unconscious defenses.

It is because she has elected and sufficiently well for the moment completed this task of self-emptying that the songwriter can exult, in St. Paul's words: "I live now not with my own life, but the life of Christ Jesus living in me." She has become Christ-filled, God-filled. In a very real sense, she has become incarnational. Using the empty vessel of her flesh, God has become incarnate through her. It is not she but God who walks in her legs, who occupies her flesh, who sings with her voice.

One morning not long after my fifteenth birthday, I spied an acquaintance walking down the road toward me. It took several minutes to traverse the distance between us. When we reached each other, we spoke briefly about schoolboy matters before we parted. A hundred yards farther down the road, I was struck by a prosaic but strangely holy realization that was to change my life.

I realized that from the time I saw him until I reached my acquaintance, all I was thinking about was what I could say that might impress him with my wit and sophistication; during our few minutes together, my attention was totally riveted on his face solely that I might judge the effectiveness of my wit, and upon his words only that I might think up the most clever possible rejoinders; and finally, during the hundred yards after I left him, I considered no issue whatsoever beyond the question of how well I had succeeded in impressing him. I realized that during that ten-minute span of time, I had been utterly preoccupied with myself. Not one brief moment was spent considering a single matter other than what I hoped might be my own possible "glory" in the other boy's eyes. Not even for a fraction of a second did I concern myself with his needs, his pain or pleasure, or any aspect of his being, except as it related to myself. In fact, he had no reality for me whatsoever beyond being a foil for my humor, beyond his potential as my admirer.

And I realized that something was seriously wrong with this state of affairs. By God's grace, I instinctively knew that this kind of consciousness was a disservice not only to my acquaintance, but to my own self. I was able to recognize that I was expending extraordinary energy—and what an enormous amount of work it was—toward an end that would ultimately be self-defeating. In one sharp, wonderful flash, I had a vision of myself continuing my same path into an incredibly pretentious, empty, and fearful old age.

So it was, by grace and for perfectly "selfish" motives, I began to take my first faltering steps on a journey toward selflessness. It has not been a quick journey. The tentacles of narcissism are subtle and penetrating and must be hacked away one by one, day after day, week after week, month after month, year after year. But what a worthwhile journey it is! For the further we proceed in diminishing our narcissism—our self-centeredness and sense of self-importance—the more we discover ourselves becoming not only less fearful of death, but also less fearful of life. No longer burdened by needs to protect our selves, we are able to lift our eyes from our selves so as to truly recognize others. And we become happier. Oh, yes, we begin to experience a sustained kind of happiness we never experienced before, as we become more self-forgetful and hence progressively more able to remember God.

I cannot pretend that I have completed the journey. But insofar as I have come, I have become free. This is what Marilyn means when she sings each chorus: "His life's blood has made you free." It is those moments when I have lost my self—when I can also sing, "I live now not with my own life"; when, like Paul, I can say, "I, Scotty, prisoner of Christ Jesus"—that I know I am most myself, that I feel most free. And then I experience some of that glory I began to stop trying to get over thirty years ago.

That's the real glory. Once you taste it you know what life is all about. But it is not your glory; it is God's. Only His. Yet, paradoxically, it is yours if you die to your self. If you humble yourself enough to truly accept that you are a creature and that He, not you, is your Creator: "Sons and daughters of His, His glory our own," Marilyn sings.

Now do you understand why I said this song was the climax? It's about real glory, and real glory is the only real climax. So, almost hidden, almost stealthily, in the quietness of her monastery, Marilyn has come into glory. Do you doubt it? Listen to the music. Listen to the tone of it reverberating with God's glory, incarnate in her singing and its substance.

I also said this song is a turning point. Where does one go after glory? To what then does one turn? It's a foolish question, because no one goes anywhere after real glory. There would be no point to it. The climax just goes on and on. But naturally, inevitably, one simply sets about revealing the glory. There's nothing else to do. And nothing else is needed.

Nonetheless, there is a certain turning reflected in the order of these songs and the flow of the subject matter. Until now the primary theme has been God's gifts to us and our openness to receiving them. But having reached the climax, as we move toward the end, the theme turns to our giving what has been given, the natural revealing or reflecting of what has been received. "Here and now we're chosen to be; to reveal His grace that all then may see."

The sparkling Christian essayist Phyllis Theroux began one of her articles as follows:

Many years ago I took a Civil Service entrance exam that contained certain questions designed to sort out the people who had "Messiah complexes" or thought that J. Edgar Hoover was giving them varicose veins. Those questions were easy to spot, although the only one that still sticks in my mind is "Do you think you are a special agent of God?" I paused, thought about all the government benefits which hung upon my answer, and wrote, "No." I would like to think that, under the same circumstances, Mr. Hoover might have lied too.[33]

To the secular, rational mind, the story of Jesus is a crazy story. The notion that God became incarnate in a carpenter's son whose brief life was ended in his execution as a petty provincial political criminal, whose body then vanished from his tomb, and whose apparition began to appear in strangely prosaic ways to the very followers who had deserted him is not a notion that will inspire faith among "sophisticated," "powerful" people. Indeed, a sort of miracle is required in the heart and mind before one can fully accept the utter reality of that bizarre story. Those of us who are recipients of this miracle feel that we are chosen "special agents." Chosen oddballs.

33. Phyllis Theroux, *The New York Times*, July 17, 1980.

"Here and now we're chosen to be; to reveal His grace that all then may see." As oddballs in this secular world of "principalities and powers" dedicated to the false gods of money and pretense, we are chosen to be special agents to live the Christ story with our very bodies until all will serve their Creator, and experience the joyful freedom of sharing His glory.

THE MARY SONG

Father, make us like Mary.
Father, fill us with grace.
Make us open and empty
To receive Your Word each day;
To give birth to Your Son;
To give birth to Your Jesus;
To give birth to Your Son;
To give Him to everyone.
Amen.

11 *Vulnerability*

VULNERABILITY IS BEGINNING TO become a fashionable word—just in the nick of time. It will be our saving grace or virtue.

As the captains of industry or the generals of armies see it—as the world sees it—vulnerability may hardly seem a virtue. It means, obviously, the ability to be wounded. But who wants to be wounded? Why would anyone desire such an ability?

Yet as I travel the nation there is one constant wherever I go—Vermont, New Jersey, California, Alabama, Kansas, North Carolina, Boston, New York City, Washington, Chicago, Dallas, Seattle, Los Angeles, country town, big city, you name it: it is the yearning for genuine community.

This yearning is most striking in the churches, since they are supposed to be communities and very seldom actually are. When I do workshops I tell the participants not to ask me questions during the break times, because most of the time their concerns are shared by other participants and should be made a part of the work of the *work*shop. Yet, invariably, a man or woman will try to seek a private conversation with me. When I remind the person of

my request, he or she is likely to respond, "But this is very important to me, and I can't talk about it in the group because some of
the members of my church are here."

I sometimes challenge that person. "How are we going to have
a decent workshop," I ask, "if the people present can't ask those
questions that are most important to them? Do you expect the others to be open and vulnerable, and you hold back? You want them
to take all the risk? Maybe if you don't take the lead, no one will. It
seems like you've got a lousy church. But what are you going to do
about it? There's no way that people can create a community—in
church or out of it—if they're not going to risk themselves with
each other. Maybe it's your responsibility as a Christian to lead
your fellow church members by being vulnerable before them."

In all fairness, if I have the opportunity, I also challenge the fellow church members. "What kind of a church do you have where
people are afraid to talk about what's most important to them?" I
inquire. "Lots of piety but not much love? Lots of backbiting but
not much honesty? Plenty of spiritual pride but little desire to be
poor in spirit? Maybe you need to ask yourselves if you are doing
something to stimulate others to fear you, to mold a fearful con-
gregation instead of encouraging a vulnerable one."

The majority of people who attend my workshops are women,
just as the majority of my patients when I practiced individual
psychotherapy were women. The men might like to think that they
are too busy working, "bringing home the bacon," for such frivoli-
ties. My own best guess, however, as to the primary reason for
this gender discrepancy is that, with respect to the psychospiri-
tual dimension of life, it is generally women who are the stronger

sex. And it is out of their strength that they are generally more able to be vulnerable than the men.

Be that as it may, I am concerned that some men may have difficulty making a song about Mary their own. Particularly when it is a song of vulnerability—of the capacity to be wounded by the Word, to be penetrated by the Spirit to the depths of one's being.

Women shouldn't have any trouble thinking in terms of being impregnated by God, nurturing Him within the emptiness of their womb, and then out of their own flesh giving birth to the Christ. But it may stretch the masculine imagination to truly identify with Mary.

By early adolescence I had become quite a decent tennis player. I had a reasonably good serve, and while my backhand was very weak, I had an extraordinarily powerful forehand. What I then did was to develop a pattern of "running around" my backhand. I would stand to the left of the center of the baseline and take every possible shot I could with my forehand. In this fashion I was able to overpower ninety-five percent of my opponents. The only problem was the other five percent. They would immediately realize my weakness, hit to my backhand, pull me farther and farther to the left side of the court, and then "crosscourt" me to my unreachable forehand and wipe *me* off the court.

At the age of thirty-two, I realized that if I was ever going to fulfill my potential as a tennis player and be the best that I could be in the game, I was going to have to work on my backhand. It was a humbling business. It meant that I had to do what had become profoundly unnatural: to stand to the right of the center of the baseline and return every possible shot with my backhand. It meant losing repeatedly to inferior players. And it meant that onlookers who had come down to the courts to watch the great Scott Peck play tennis watched him hit balls two courts down or over the fence or into the net. But within three months I had a decent backhand for the first time in my life, and with a whole tennis game, I became the best player in the little island community where I lived. At which point, I began to take up golf. That was really humbling.

The point is that if we are to progress in the "game" of life, we need to work on our weak sides. More often than not our sexuality is like my adolescent tennis style; we men tend to run around our femininity, just as women tend to avoid exercising their masculine qualities. We are called to be whole people. The words "health," "wholeness," and "holiness," as I have said, all have the same root. It is both our psychological and spiritual task, particularly during the second half of our life, to work toward androgyny. Androgyny is neither like bisexuality nor some unisexed compromise; it is, like a whole tennis game, the fullest expression of our potential, the best that we can be. So it is in their journey toward health and wholeness and holiness I find that I must teach most of my male patients how to be women, and most of my female patients how to be men.

It is therefore particularly meaningful and important for us men to pray, "Father, make us like Mary." And to remember that, in the words of C. S. Lewis, "in relation to God we are all feminine."[34] Remember also that in my meditation on worship I spoke

---

34. C. S. Lewis, *That Hideous Strength* (New York: Macmillan, 1965), p. 316.

of how we are commanded to love God *totally*—with all our heart and all our mind and all our soul. Total love is not passionless.

Male or female, we can do no better than to echo the words of John Donne from his Holy Sonnet number 14:

> Batter my heart, three-personed God . . .
> Take me to You, imprison me, for I,
> Except You enthrall me, never shall be free
> Nor ever chaste, except You ravish me.

It is just this kind of total passionate love that is required for us to be "impregnated by God" so that we might "give birth" to His son. But what is meant by giving birth to Jesus? We have spoken of giving birth to Jesus within ourselves, of becoming so God-filled that we can say: "I live now not with my own life, but with Jesus living in me." But how is the delivery into the external world accomplished? How do we "give Him to everyone"?

No forceps are required. Once we totally love God, once we become genuinely full of Christ, we quite naturally begin to behave like him. The Word flows out of us not in pious words, but in quiet action. The second great commandment is "like unto" the first, and it comes easily to love our neighbors as ourselves, to forgive them their trespasses, even to love our enemies. This can be done only from a position of psychological maturity or strength. Remember how I commented it is out of this kind of strength that women are generally more able to be vulnerable than men. It is no accident that I had to reach the age of thirty-two before I could be humble enough and mature and powerful enough to display my weakness, as was required to work on my backhand. Still, let's be really specific.

Mature Christians are called to disarm. If Jesus taught us anything, he taught us that the way to salvation is through our vulnerability. He opened himself to the poor, the prostitutes, the lepers, the cripples, the foreigners, the outcasts, the untouchables. And when the time came that he would be delivered unto death, he raised no hand except to receive the killing wounds of the Establishment. So it is that the theologian Dorothy Solle has referred to Jesus as "God's unilateral disarmament."

Good theology always makes good psychology. What happens when one person says to another: "I'm confused, I'm not sure where I'm going; I'm feeling lost and lonely; I'm tired and frightened. Will you help me?" The effect of such vulnerability is almost invariably disarming. "I'm lonely and tired too," others are likely to say, and open up to us. But what happens if we try to maintain a macho image of having it all together, of being the top dog, when we gird ourselves about with our psychological defenses? We become unapproachable, and our neighbors gird themselves in their defenses, and our human relationships become no more meaningful or productive than empty tanks bumping together in the night.

Father, make us like Mary.

The policy of our predominantly and supposedly Christian country is to be as invulnerable as conceivably possible. Granted that other nations, Christian or Jewish or Muslim or Hindu, capitalist or Communist, are also as frantically trying to be as invulnerable as the United States, but who is it that is going to lead us out of this mess?

Rather than explore avenues of creative vulnerability, we are utterly dedicated to maintaining a supermasculine image of impregnable raw power and imposing, overweening confidence that can admit no weakness. The nation whose coinage proclaims "In God We Trust" is the world's leading manufacturer of weapons.

Father, make us like Mary.

When I think of all that is required to bring an end to the arms race—not only changes in individual styles and attitudes, but the willingness of the military-industrial establishment to no longer worship Mammon, and the willingness of the nation to relinquish its external sovereignty to a supranational agency—it seems to me that a virtual Second Coming is required. In fact, that is what it is all about. With all due respect to the traditional millennialists, I think what is meant by the Second Coming is not the bodily return of Jesus, but the coming of the mystical body of his True Church—the coming of the spirit of Christ to everyone, sweeping through the nation, sweeping through the world.

Father, make us like Mary . . . to give birth to Your Son; to give him to everyone.

This *is* the time of the Second Coming, whether we like it or not. There's no alternative except self-annihilation. And the battle is heating up just as predicted. The forces of evil are coming out into the open. The iron fists within the velvet gloves are about to be revealed as the wealthy of the world who become wealthier while the impoverished masses become poorer. And we must face the fact that crucifixion is not something that happened to that one man nineteen hundred and fifty years ago. They're going to want to stone us again. And ultimately, what "giving birth" to Jesus means is that we need to be willing to die for love and truth.

I'm sorry. I know it sounds hard. It is hard. But there's no escaping it. It is the time of the Second Coming. "Here and now we're chosen to be, to reveal His grace that all then may see." It's either give birth to Jesus or face the consequences. The time to choose is upon us.

Father, make us like Mary.

WHAT RETURN CAN I MAKE?

(Based on Psalm 116)

I love for the Lord hears my prayer.
He stoops to listen to my plea,
And when death comes close, distress and anguish fill me
I call upon His name.
And He is always there.

Our God, You are tender, full of compassion.
You lift Your children from their knees.
You dry their tears and place them in Your presence;
They call upon Your name
And You are always there.

Rest my soul, the Lord has been good to you.
Your God has freed you from all fear.
He has saved you from death, He's kept your feet from stumbling.
Just call upon His name.
And He is always there.

I am Your servant, O Lord.
And all my vows to You I will pay.
In the presence of Your people, I'll offer You thanksgiving
And call upon Your name,
For You are always there.

What return can I make to the Lord for His goodness to me?
I will drink of His saving cup and call upon His name.
I will drink of Your saving cup and call upon Your name.

12 Returning

RETURNING IS A WORD with many meanings. We can return home or to a favorite haunt. We can return a piece of defective merchandise. But here Marilyn and I are using it to mean "giving back."

Many think of giving as something other than returning. If I give a toy to a child, I'm not paying him or her back, am I? If I give money to charity, more often than not it is to one that has not ever supported me. Yet think for a moment. I talk about "my" children as if they were my property—as if I had earned them or created them. Similarly, I refer to our five acres as "my" land, even though it's been farmed by ten generations of white men before me and dozens of generations of Native Americans before them. Are they "my" flowers that grace our gardens? Or are they a gift to me? Certainly I do not know how to make a flower. I know only how to cultivate one. When I water my flowers, am I giving to them, or am I simply returning to the land a small bit of what it has given to me? So it is at the conclusion of the offering in the church service—when the plate with all our little bills and weekly envelopes is brought to the altar—we ritually and quite properly say, "All things come of Thee, O Lord, and of Thine own have we given Thee."

"All things come of Thee, O Lord." Our children. Our land. Our money. Even our own lives. In the last meditation on vulnerability, I spoke of how crucifixion is not something that only Jesus and the earliest Christians had to think about. Although it may require extraordinary courage and suffering, the reality is that dying in God's service is merely returning to Him what He has given. Still, I could not ask you to be willing to die with me in God's service if death were the end of it all. But of course it isn't.

Of course?

Writing about the song "In Quest of Wisdom," I noted how the development of personal religion is rooted in the personal struggle with the mystery of death. In "A New Song," Marilyn sang Christ's words "Ask and you will receive. Seek and you will find. Knock and it will be opened to you." I have hardly got the mystery of death—much less the Mystery of God—wrapped up in a neat intellectual package. But, after struggling with it since adolescence, I have received and found enough for the mystery to be sufficiently opened to me to be able to say, "Of course death is not the end of the human spirit."

People sometimes ask me, "Dr. Peck, who was the most influential writer in your life?" I wish I could say Plato or Aristotle or St. Thomas Aquinas, but the fact of the matter is that I made it through college by going to those sleazy bookstores where you could buy synopses of Plato and Aristotle or the equivalent of St. Thomas Aquinas Classic Comics. To be honest, I was far more influenced by a pre-TV family sitcom book entitled *Cheaper by the Dozen*. It was about two parents who were "efficiency experts" and their twelve children. I had never heard of an efficiency expert before, and after reading this delightful book as a child in the late 1940s, I decided to be an efficiency expert when I grew up. And by God's grace, that is just what I have become. Neuroses and other varieties of human ignorance are inefficient. First as a psychotherapist and more lately as an evangelist to boot, I have been in a position to teach people to live their lives more efficiently. We can obviously live efficiently only in accord, in harmony, with reality. Insofar as humans continue to live disharmoniously by struggling against the Real, our existence remains inefficient.

I have become sufficiently professional in my work that I am filled with admiration for those who do it better than I. The reader may remember that in my meditation on grace, I exclaimed, "God's efficiency never ceases to amaze me. Not a wasted motion!" And when I think of the energy—the love—that God pours into the development of each individual soul, I know that there is no death for the human spirit.

Remember that fearful woman who learned how to close her eyes while jogging and exulted, "To think that the Creator of the whole universe would take the time to go running with me!"

Forget about all the so-called evidence of an afterlife—near-death experiences, for example. Once we begin to know God, it is simply unreasonable to think that we should be born only to die. For the past decade, my wife, Lily, and I have laboriously nurtured a flower bed in our yard from its first planting to its present magnificence. Do you think that now we would take a flame-thrower to it or bulldoze it? Of course not! Such inefficiency would be insane. So it is with God. Most things about Him I don't begin to comprehend; but wasteful and unloving He is not.

I do not mean to tell you that dying is easy—least of all dying before one's time. If dying were easy, there would be no sacrifice. I merely mean that it is not the end. This is why Marilyn sings, "Your God has freed you from all fear. He has saved you from death." Not only can we deduce from God's love that there is no extinction of the soul, but to prove the point, He sent his Son to first live as one of us, then to die as one of us, and finally to walk in spirit among us once again. Nowhere is this love better expressed than in the writings of John Claypool, here recalling his sudden insight into the meaning of resurrection:

I can still remember the time when this aspect of the Easter story hit me with full intensity. For the purpose of illustration, I began to imagine that a certain tenant family was having all kinds of problems, and I had resolved to do what I could to help them. I arranged to have them move onto some land I owned, and into a house that I provided. I went out and tried to teach them skills that went with making a living on a farm, and I provided the money for the seed and the equipment for farming. I set them up so at last they could have a chance to live creatively. But very soon it became apparent that these persons were not responding positively to what I had done. They were not working. They were wrecking the house that I had provided them. They were tearing up the machinery and using the money intended for seed to buy liquor. However, I did not give up. I continued to reason with them. I sent out the county agent and other people who might be able to help, and patiently stayed with my goal of helping these people out of the condition they had gotten themselves into. But things only got worse.

Finally, in my imagination, my only son said to me, "Perhaps there is a way I can get to them. They know who I am. I have a special feel for some of the younger members of the family. Perhaps if I went out and spent some time with them, we could reverse the trend and get them on the right track."

And so, with no small misgiving, I agreed to let him go. And two days later word came back, "They took your son in and received him cordially at first. But then very quickly their mood changed, and they became sullen and hostile. Just yesterday they took him out behind the barn, tied his hands and tortured him for a while, and then killed him in cold blood."

As I allowed myself to feel the emotions of such a situation, I found a primitive rage building up in me against the creatures who would do this sort of thing. My first impulse was to unleash all the hurtful and destructive powers within me against such utter ingrates. I had to admit that if it had been in my power to raise my son back from the dead, it would never in a thousand years have occurred to me to send him back to the kind of creatures who had treated him this way.

At that point, the miracle of the Easter event broke over me. It was not just the power of God that astonished me here—the ability to take something that had been killed and call it back to life again. That is amazing. But even more amazing is the patience and mercy of a God who would still have hope for the kind of creatures who had treated his only begotten Son that way. Three days after human beings killed him in cold blood, the word was out, not only that he was alive again, but that he was saying, "I go before you into Galilee. Let's keep on keeping on. Let's get back to the task of dispelling suspicion and reconciling the world back to the Father as he really is." That is the towering miracle of Easter that broke in on me that day.[35]

---

35. John Claypool, *The Preaching Event* (Waco, TX: Word, 1980).

What should our proper response be to such love? The answer is obvious: gratitude. A few years ago at a symposium with theologian Theodore Gill, I commented that a sense of gratitude was one of the characteristics of any genuine Christian. Ted countered by saying, "Gratitude is not one of the characteristics; it is the primary characteristic." Indeed, gratitude is so basic it is like salvation itself: paradoxically both the rational result of effort and the unearned gift of grace.

It is easy for me to be grateful; my parents worked hard to give me the best education, the experience of travel, and many little luxuries to boot, and most important, they cared for me personally and emotionally. I do not think my gratitude is an accident. Yet the truth is that some who come from backgrounds as nurturing as mine often end up as chronic complainers, never satisfied, always feeling cheated. Others, however, even though the victims of the grossest deprivation and oppression, grow to have words of praise and thanksgiving almost continually on their lips. It is mysterious.

But oh so important! In a movie full of despair, *Cool Hand Luke,* I recall the warden saying to the prisoner, Luke, "Boy, you got an attitude problem." Although the warden was a brutal and ugly man—clearly the villain of the piece—he was correct in his assessment not only of Luke, who did have a fatal chip on his shoulder, but also of virtually everyone. As a psychotherapist, I could have healed all my patients quickly had I the power to change their attitudes. Those of my patients who have been healed, however, did so because they managed—somehow by God's grace and their own painstaking, slow labor in submission to the psychotherapeutic discipline and process—to heal themselves by altering their attitudes to conform with a larger reality.

So it is that if I could have but one prayer to make on behalf of my parents, my friends, or anyone anywhere, I would pray that they receive the gift of a grateful heart. The attitude of gratitude is the very beginning of the Christian experience. In some ways it is also the end; for out of the grateful heart so many things naturally evolve, such as praise. I am reminded of the concluding verse of that famous hymn of Christian gratitude "Amazing Grace":

> And when we've been there ten thousand years
> Bright shining as the sun
> We'll have no less days to sing God's praise
> Than when we first begun.

It is no accident, therefore, that Marilyn's song of gratitude and praise is the finale or that its title is the expression of something else that naturally evolves out of the grateful heart: the sense of obligation. You have given me so much, dear Lord. What can I give back in return?

What God wants back is our love. Remember the first of Christ's two great commandments: "Love the Lord, your God, with all your heart and soul and mind." God does not want perfunctory praise any more than burnt offerings; He wants the true adoration of total passionate love. He wants our total commitment.

But how is such love to be manifest? I took great pains in *The Road Less Traveled* to make it clear that love is not a feeling. Genuine love is always manifested in loving behavior. It is not a matter of empty words; it is a matter of deeds. My grandfather was a case in point.

I was blessed with the kind of grandfather every boy should have. A simple man, he was not given to eloquence. Indeed, his speech often seemed to be little more than a series of hackneyed phrases and sayings. "Don't put all your eggs in one basket," he advised me. "If wishes were horses, beggars would ride," he said, over and again.

Not all his proverbial admonishments were harsh. Hardly. "All work and no play makes Jack a dull boy" was one of his favorites. "Sometimes it's better to be a big fish in a small pond than a little fish in a big pond" was another.

I can't say that I always enjoyed his almost constant stream of platitudes. If I heard "All that glitters is not gold" once, I heard it a thousand times. My grandfather was not above repeating himself.

But he loved me. Once a month or so during my pre-TV prepubescent years, I went across Manhattan to visit him for the weekend. At my request, my visit never varied. He always took me to a movie double feature on Saturday afternoon. Following dinner, we always went to another double feature that night. The movie theaters then, in deference to God, were usually closed on Sunday mornings. But we always attended yet a third double feature on Sunday afternoon before he sent me off back home. On each thirty-hour visit, he sat through six movies with me. That was love.

Consequently—given to me during intermissions and our walks back and forth to the theaters—my grandfather's sayings, unexciting though they might have been to a ten-year-old boy, were made quite palatable for my digestion, while simultaneously teaching me how to live. "A spoonful of sugar makes the medicine go down," he himself would have put it. My grandfather gave me a whole lot of sugar.

"I am your servant, O Lord," Marilyn sings. How do we serve God? How do we translate our love into action? Just what is it that God wants us to do? Marilyn has already given us the answer in "Prayer for the Kingdom." God wants us to bring His kingdom into being.

We will not bring the kingdom into being by clobbering people over the head with it, any more than we will by attempting to manipulate other countries with our military "gifts" or threats. "Handsome is as handsome does," my grandfather would have said. The Inquisitors who tortured their victims on the rack and burned them at the stake were not loving them "as themselves." God's true "special agents" work as quietly and gently as my grandfather—taking children to the movies, stopping to help a stranger fix a flat tire, praying for an enemy, addressing envelopes for a peace organization.

So the return we can make is to love our neighbors as ourselves—Christ's second commandment, which he said was "like unto" the first. God has literally given us life. To revere Him is to revere the gift and hence develop what Albert Schweitzer called "reverence for life." To nurture life is our obligation. We cannot love God without assuming it. We are called to nurture ourselves. We are called to nurture our children and our grandchildren. We are also called to nurture the Russians and the Ethiopians and the Vietnamese, the wolves and the whales, the beaches and the forests, the whole fecund panoply of God's creation.

Jesus commanded his disciples, "Love one another as I have loved you." And shortly afterward he died for us. Did he really mean that we too should be prepared to die for the Russians and the whales and the forests? Yes, he did mean that. Some of us who are disciples will sooner or later find ourselves in a position where we cannot simultaneously be faithful to God and save our skins. We will be obliged to return the bodies he gave us. The time for Christian martyrs has not yet passed. If that time should happen to come for you, you will know that Jesus paved the way and went to prepare a place for you. And you will have some faith, however dim, by virtue of your experience of God's love, that death is only a veil and martyrdom yet another God-given opportunity.

Most of us, however, will be called to the long haul. My grandfather faded away (returned) at ninety-two as gently as he lived. Like him, we will find it our obligation to serve God in the world until the fatigue becomes more than we can bear. And then what a welcoming there will be!

Epilogue

THIS WORK HAS BEEN dedicated to the Glory of God

The glory of God cannot be captured.

Of the God-Christ, symbolized by a lion, C. S. Lewis remarked, "He's wild, you know."[36] He cannot be captured. God is not ours to control, we are His to control. He comes to us in His time and in His way.

We can only capture that which has dimensions. But God is beyond dimensions. This is why Eastern mystics will sometimes refer to God as nothingness or emptiness—the "God of the Void"—not to deny His reality, but to affirm His "beyondness."

Still, God comes to us leaping along the dimensions of sight and sound, thought and touch, smell and feeling . . . and we get caught by glimpses of the glory. Sometimes we break away, frightened, fighting to forget that anything could be so important. Others of us stay with it, and then find nothing else important enough to talk about. As the first song of this book says: "And all we could do was sing of the Lord."

36. C. S. Lewis, *The Lion, the Witch and the Wardrobe* (New York: Macmillan, 1950).

How much all this singing and talking of the Lord helps, we do not know. We recognize it to be a compulsion.

> And whosoever in his heart has heard
> That music, all his life shall toil to say
> The passion of it. But there is no word—
> No words are made for it. There is no way.[37]

Nonetheless, we keep trying. So we have here yet another work of evangelism, attempting once again to somehow transit—this time through the combined dimensions of music and prose—the dimensionless grandeur of God.

That all may know Him and rejoice.

---

37. John Hall Wheelock, "Unison," in *This Blessed Earth: New and Selected Poems 1927–1977* (New York: Scribner's, 1978).

Acknowledgments

The author gratefully acknowledges permission to reprint the following:

Excerpt from *The Night and Nothing* by Gale D. Webbe, copyright © 1964 by Gale D. Webbe. Reprinted by permission of Harper & Row Publishers, Inc.

Excerpt from *The Family Reunion* by T. S. Eliot, copyright © 1939 by T. S. Eliot; renewed 1967 by Esme Valerie Eliot. Reprinted by permission of Harcourt Brace Jovanovich, Inc.

Excerpt from "The Love Song of J. Alfred Prufrock" in *Collected Poems 1909–1962* by T. S. Eliot, copyright © 1936 by Harcourt Brace Jovanovich, Inc.; copyright © 1963, 1964 by T. S. Eliot. Reprinted by permission of the publisher.

Excerpt from *Murder in the Cathedral* by T. S. Eliot, copyright © 1935 by Harcourt Brace Jovanovich, Inc.; renewed 1963 by T. S. Eliot. Reprinted by permission of the publisher.

Excerpt from *Power Through Acceptance: The Secret of Serenity* by Gordon Powell, copyright © 1977 by Gordon Powell; published by Christian Herald Books. Reprinted by permission of the author.

Excerpt from *Chicago Poems* by Carl Sandberg, copyright © 1916 by Holt, Rinehart & Winston, Inc.; renewed 1944 by Carl Sandberg. Reprinted by permission of Harcourt Brace Jovanovich, Inc.

Excerpt from an article by Phyllis Theroux that first appeared in *The New York Times*. Reprinted by permission of the author.